"If You Lean In,

Will Men Just
Look Down
Your Blouse?"

Also by Gina Barreca

It's Not That I'm Bitter . . . : Or How I Learned to Stop Worrying About Visible Panty Lines and Conquered the World

Babes in Boyland: A Personal History of Co-Education in the Ivy League

I'm with Stupid: One Man . . . One Woman . . . 10,000 Years of Misunderstanding Between the Sexes Cleared Right Up, co-written with Gene Weingarten

The ABC of Vice: An Insatiable Women's Guide, Alphabetized, co-written with cartoonist Nicole Hollander

Too Much of a Good Thing Is Wonderful

Sweet Revenge: The Wicked Delights of Getting Even

Untamed and Unabashed: Essays on Women and Humor in British Literature

Perfect Husbands (& Other Fairy Tales): Demystifying Marriage, Men, and Romance

They Used to Call Me Snow White . . . But I Drifted: Women's Strategic Use of Humor

Edited by Gina Barreca

Make Mine a Double: Why Women Like Us Like to Drink* (*or Not)

Vital Ideas: Sex

The Signet Book of American Humor

Don't Tell Mama! The Penguin Book of Italian American Writing

A Sitdown with the Sopranos: Watching Italian American Culture on TV's Most Talked-About Series

The Erotics of Instruction, co-edited with Deborah Denenholz Morse

The Penguin Book of Women's Humor

Desire and Imagination: 20 Classic Essays in Sexuality

Women of the Century: Thirty Modern Short Stories

Fay Weldon's Wicked Fictions

New Perspectives on Women and Comedy

Sex and Death in Victorian Literature

Last Laughs: Perspectives on Women and Comedy

GINA BARRECA

"If You Lean In,

Will Men Just Look Down Your Blouse?"

*Questions and Thoughts
for Loud, Smart Women
in Turbulent Times*

ST. MARTIN'S PRESS ᴍ NEW YORK

[handwritten inscription: 2017 For Renée! Here's to laughter! Gina]

For the woman who rides the subway to the end of the line.
For the woman who wakes up in the middle of the night.
For the woman who spills out, spills over, overdoes it,
and can't contain herself.
For the Tribe of Loud, Smart, Funny Women—
(and for the men who laugh with us).

A number of these essays have appeared in earlier forms in the *Hartford Courant*,
Psychology Today, and *The Chronicle of Higher Education*.

www.stmartins.com

The Library of Congress Cataloging-in-Publication Data is available
upon request.

ISBN 978-1-250-06074-7 (hardcover)
ISBN 978-1-4668-6638-6 (e-book)

First Edition: March 2016

10 9 8 7 6 5 4 3 2 1

CONTENTS

Contents

Contents

PART 4. HE DIDN'T LEAD ME INTO TEMPTATION:
WE TOOK A SHORTCUT

Contents

PART 5. IF YOU RUN WITH A BAD CROWD, CAN YOU CALL IT EXERCISE?

PART 6. IF YOU MET MY FAMILY, YOU'D UNDERSTAND

Contents

PART 1

I'm Not Needy; I'm Wanty

1

Does Beauty Really Equal Bondage?
or "How I Learned to Stop Worrying
and Loathe the Spanx"

Could you be talked into purchasing a foundation undergarment so restrictive, so unyielding, and so draconian it makes a wetsuit look like a nightgown?

Here's why I ask: There's been a pop-up (rarely has the term been so grievously misused) ad appearing in the lower right-hand screen of my computer which at first seemed merely persistent but turned out to have been irresistible. It offered me a product that would, through cunning and science, give me a better figure. This week, I relented. Casting my integrity to the wind, I clicked on the link.

What I saw made me gasp, then wince, then toss my head and offer the hollow laughter of film sirens who discovered their boyfriends were no-good, gunslinging liars. The website was selling girdles. They didn't call them that, but that's what they were.

A girdle is a girdle is a girdle.

I grew up watching early women's rights activists burn their bras and girdles. Now times have changed and women are putting their undergarments into the flames for a different reason: They're doing it to forge the steel infrastructure more thoroughly by placing them in the refiner's fire.

That's why they're called foundation garments—they're made of metal and concrete. They're supposed to support the whole structure, from the bottom-up and the inside-out.

These new products differ from the girdles worn by women of my mother's generation only insofar as there are now girdles for the legs, girdles for the arms, and girdles for an adult's entire body. Turns out you don't just have to flatten your stomach anymore. You have to flatten your whole self.

I started looking at various other links for women's foundation garments—there are more than 28 million entries, so I narrowed my search to the first 75,000—and it seems as if the most popular brand at the moment is a product called Spanx.

Name aside, I don't believe this product has anything to do with the act of spanking because, as far as I can tell, the hand of the person attempting such an act would ricochet off the taut trampoline-like surface of the fabric and in all probability cause the spanker to put out an eye or cause severe damage to his (or her, but you know it would be his) wrist.

In some cases, of course, that would be appropriate.

But what might start out as playful could become deadly and we should all remember that, especially before wearing an item of clothing that resembles a lace-edged iron maiden.

The premise behind Spanx is this: if you put Jell-O into a Thermos, it won't remember it's Jell-O.

This realization did not prevent me from wondering whether I might not be wise to purchase one. I've always been fond of Thermoses, which are the cleverest of appliances. You put in a hot beverage, it keeps it hot; you put in a cold beverage, it keeps it cold. As the old joke goes, "How do(es) it know?" But so-called shapewear? It turns out it's not so intelligent. That's why smart broads were eager to shed it.

Today's advertising rhetoric says shapewear will "smooth" your silhouette, which sounds rather comforting and benign, but with a little research (reading another 48,000 articles) a person can start to believe in conspiracy theories concerning the deviousness of underwear manufacturers rivaling those put forth by flat-world theorists—with the same impulse to get rid of curves.

Researchers argue that these arcane garments will cut off the circulation of blood to several of your favorite major organs—especially those having to do with digestion—and cause reflux, heartburn, and flatulence.

Fabulous, right? The fabric is virtually airtight; the wearer is trapped inside a Spanx garment. She is burping, belching, and releasing enough natural gas to keep the lights on in Tulsa for a three-day weekend, but the vapors are sealed in.

So now picture these ladies—smooth ladies, every one of them—slowly wafting toward the ceiling at the end of a gala, rising with a kind of grand elegance until they are gently bobbing up there against the lighting fixtures like balloons.

Surely at some point they, and their self-esteem, deflate and return to earth?

So you'll not be surprised I decided to skip the equation that beauty equals bondage, even when it's trying to pass itself off as a textile buttress.

Women don't need to bring back the whalebone in our corsets; what we need is to develop enough backbone to shed them altogether.

2

Unlearning the Kindergarten Lessons of Life

Like almost every other woman I know, many of the lessons I've had to unlearn in life I first learned in kindergarten.

For example, I've had to break the habit of having cookies and a nap at three in the afternoon.

That's because as an adult I developed this fetish about wanting to hold a steady job and not take up so much physical space I need to be hauled around by a winch.

Lying down every day after a heavy sugar and carb intake can undermine a girl's ambitions as well as her ability to enter a room without turning sideways and breathing in.

After a certain age, I also had to learn to stop automatically holding the hand of the person walking next to me. I discovered in my mid- to late twenties (I'm a slow learner) that the unoccupied hand belonging to my "buddy" (or boyfriend, or first husband) was often furtively engaged in holding a miniature bottle of cinnamon schnapps, the keys to a vehicle he didn't own, or the hand of another wide-eyed girl. (Sometimes all three. Remember: slow learner.)

One of the biggest revelations came when I realized that I did not have to share everything. That was fascinating. To believe I could be a good girl and yet insist that some stuff belonged only to me? It was hard to convince myself that somebody else wanting a piece of what I've got (a piece of pie, a piece of the action, a piece of my heart, whatever) was not a reason to fork it over. I was in my forties when I learned that even if somebody asks nicely, it is OK to say no.

Over the years, I've also had to learn that life is not a game of tag (nowhere is "safe") and that in most workplaces time-outs are not the penalty for behaving badly. I also discovered, along with the rest of America, that although in politics, professional sports, and Hollywood there are no penalties for behaving badly, if you're working retail or for a corporation you'll be fired before you can say, "I'm sorry."

Lately, though, I've realized that I've clung to the schematics behind the game of Duck, Duck, Goose as a guiding force for far too long. In women's lives especially (and since I'm talking about the pre-K demographic I'll call us girls without fear of appearing patronizing), all sorts of lessons have encouraged us to sit politely and wait to be chosen. Remember the game Duck, Duck, Goose, where you sat in a circle facing the center and waited to be recognized as the "goose," whereupon you were tapped and permitted to run around making choices yourself?

And how many fairy tales taught us essentially the same lesson? "Duck, Duck, Cinderella!" "Duck, Duck, Snow White!" Or classic books? "Duck, Duck, Madame Bovary!" "Duck, Duck, Anna Karenina!" Or popular movies? "Duck, Duck, Julia Roberts playing a hooker in *Pretty Woman*!"

Great lesson, right? Learn to win at a game where ritual passivity is preparation for random selection? Where the goal is to be distinguished as exceptional, not presumably because you possess any duck-like attributes (God forbid), but because you're not paying attention and might be a slow runner? Learn how to play a game where the object is to get caught?

Boys are rewarded for playing games where they line up by height and then run into walls. Perhaps I'm making that up—or perhaps you should do a Google search for "Guy Runs into Wall for Fun."

If you do, you'll notice that the recent number of visits to that YouTube page is about 3.5 million. The official YouTube page for the Olympics, in contrast? Fewer than a million views. And the YouTube page for the National Women's History Museum's video titled *Three Generations Fighting for the Vote*? Fifty-six views, total.

Men and women alike have to examine the lessons we teach—even for fun—and rewrite the rules of the games we play.

Nobody wants to go through life as the guy who slams into walls. And nobody wants to spend her life as a sitting duck.

3

The Cheap-Motel Backside of Facebook

Wouldn't it be just absolutely great if people put snapshots of themselves at their most miserable—not cute miserable, but *actually* miserable—on Facebook?

Real life, as we all know, is like seeing the reverse side of a perfectly executed needlepoint: it's messy, it's chaotic, and it's tough to see the big picture.

Years ago, a friend introduced me to what he calls the Miserable Snapshot Theory of Life. Since people now upload daily, sometimes hourly, photographs of fabulous meals, beautiful children, and astonishing vacations as evidence of their unimpeachably happy existences, his theory has even more appeal than it did originally.

Here's the premise: What if, when we were young, we could look into our future and see only the most ridiculous, awkward, and pitiful sequences? What would we think about ourselves then?

And now I'll tell you one of my pitiful moments, which starts as if it were an ordinary story: My husband and I drove across the country. We had a safe car, audiobooks, and enough cash to stay indoors. We were ready for fun.

Yes, parts of the trip were Facebook gleeful: diners with

perfectly crisp hash; a local rodeo in Montana; landscapes so stark we wouldn't have been surprised to see a triceratops walk across the road.

But then there was this one night in Northern California.

It rained hard all day and driving had been tough: windshield wipers on, difficult to see the road, some pretty serious fog. We were going to try to make it farther north but decided around seven to call it quits. We pulled into a small city and chose a small local motel, since the plan was to get some serious sleep and leave early the next day.

Fair enough, right? So far, so good. So what if there were no other vehicles in the parking lot? Maybe the staff all walked to work. It was the West Coast. They're very health-conscious out there.

And OK, the room was a little worse than usual. For starters, it had a neon orange shag rug that had seen better days as far back as, say, 1972. I thought I heard crickets coming from inside the rug, but I convinced myself that my hearing was playing tricks on me. The shag couldn't be so deep that it had its own ecosystem, surely.

The room's only attempt at decoration consisted of six faded clown prints fully bolted to the walls. This implied that other guests had attempted to steal them.

There were twin beds covered by nylon paisley bedspreads so slippery that it was nearly impossible not to slide off directly onto the shag rug, thereby becoming consumed by whatever lived within its layers.

Seeing the expression on my face, Michael said, "I'll go get us some food."

The understanding was that, while he was gone, I would unpack whatever we needed, open the wine, and get our evening started. I looked around for those little plastic glasses usually on shelves in the bathroom. Not only were there no cups in the bathroom; there were no shelves.

There was, however, another clown print. But no cups, no glasses.

I decided to drink the wine regardless.

My husband returned to find his wife sitting on a nylon paisley bed drinking cheap wine directly out of the bottle while gazing stupefied at Bozo.

In a falsely cheerful voice Michael announced, "The only thing I could find to eat was potato salad."

"Where did you get potato salad where there was no other food?" I asked.

"There was a deli, it was closing, and I didn't like the look of the cold cuts."

I started rifling through the paper bag for napkins and cutlery. There were napkins, but no spoons, knives, or forks.

"Michael," I asked, "how are we supposed to eat this?"

"What do you mean?" he said.

"There are no implements," I pointed out.

In a phrase I at first didn't understand, Michael said, "I have a shoehorn." He looked enormously pleased with himself.

Then I got it. So we sat at the ends of our respective beds, passing the bottle back and forth along with the plastic container of potato salad as we shoveled food into our mouths with a shoehorn.

Let's face it: If you'd told me when I was a kid, "Honey, you're gonna spend a night sitting in a sleazy motel eating potato salad with a shoehorn and staring at a clown print in silence," would I have really worked so hard in college?

I used to think I'd like to see my future: "Oh if only I could fast-forward a little bit, and see where I end up, that will give me motivation to do well, and be all that I can be!"

Right.

We have to choose those snapshots carefully. None of them are representative: it's all about context.

When Michael and I left the next morning, our drive took us though fields of orchids. Had we not stopped the night before, we would have driven past them in the dark.

A picture might be worth a thousand words, but you choose your words and your pictures carefully.

And always pack a shoehorn.

4

Women Carry Everything We Need to Start Life in a New State

Not only do women hold up half the sky; we do it while carrying a 500-pound purse.

Women carry with us, at all times, everything we might need to start life in a new state. Our purses contain all the merchandise found in a Kwik-E-Mart or a bodega.

Men? Men carry a credit card and a twenty. If they need it, they buy it. Or they ask us for it.

After all, we'll have it in our bag.

We carry extra eyeglasses, lip balm, Q-tips, Band-Aids, a half-empty water bottle, four pens (two of which work), sixteen crumpled receipts, a tiny notebook, gum, mints, hand sanitizer, perfume sample (empty), tampon, aspirin, non-aspirin pain relievers, Tums, Imodium, matches (we don't smoke; they're for friends), a "fun-size" Snickers, nail glue, an emery board, a compact 5X mirror (ironic, right?), tweezers, a cell phone, Bluetooth, floss, a AAA battery (which helps with nothing, ever), and three cute, striped paper clips too adorable to discard.

We also have a folded article we're going to read as soon as we get a minute, an address book (I don't trust technology—I like to have it written down somewhere), calendar (ditto), an encouraging fortune from a cookie ("Forget the doubts and fears creeping into your life. The universe is guiding you!"), a packet of cheap tissues, a packet of nicer tissues (for other people), a note from our niece ("I love you THIS much!"), and one earring.

Every woman over thirty has, at the very bottom of her bag, a lipstick that she got as part of a "Free Gift" from Clinique in 2007 that she's *never* worn, but who in her right mind would ever throw out a perfectly good lipstick from Clinique? Yet we don't want it cluttering up our bathroom. So we carry it, talisman-like, and go around offering it to strange women, saying with false conviction, "I think you'd look great in this color!"

We stock up. Once before doing a talk on humor and wellness at an elite medical conference, I walked around the vendors' area to see what items they offered as bait to lure attendees to their booths. I find some of these treasures particularly alluring; I once came home with, no kidding, a Viagra clock. I laugh when it reaches noon.

At this conference, however, one company was giving away medicated bandages in small plastic containers bearing their logo. Nice, right? Practical, sensible, and inexpensive.

And for twenty minutes I watched as elegantly dressed, name-badged women from the medical industry, the insurance industry, and huge pharmaceutical companies who, in Armani suits and with Fendi purses, scooped up those plastic containers as if they'd never seen an adhesive strip before.

They could be heard justifying themselves as they grabbed handfuls: "I'll keep this in the car." "I'm putting this in Zack's knapsack." "Good for traveling." Some were sliding the containers directly into those Fendi bags. They wore the same glazed expressions as Doomsday preppers.

I did not see one man—not one, mind you—take this particular trophy.

Guys were taking baseball caps, pens, flashlights, and pedometers, so it wasn't as if they were averse to the process.

They simply steered clear of the non-fun items, which, of course, they could rely on the women around them to have.

C'mon, would you ever consider going up to a guy and asking if he had a Band-Aid? Or some ibuprofen?

In fact, if you went up to a man and said, "You wouldn't have any pain reliever on you, would you?" he'd recoil. He'd assume that you were nuts or that you mistook him for a drug dealer—and not from a pharmaceutical company.

Women get asked this kind of thing constantly and we feel guilty if we can't say yes. One morning I was muttering about missing my coffee. A stranger reached into her bag, gave me a cardboard container of hot coffee, and apologized because it might not be the way I take it. I'm just sorry now that I didn't say I was hungry—she would have pulled out a pan of baked ziti.

Women: Isn't it time for us to lighten our burdens, dump the junk, and use our shoulders for the real work of the world? Also, would you like this lipstick? You'd look great in it.

5

The $150,000 Park Avenue Purse

There's a new book giving primates a bad name. It's not doing women much good, either.

Primates of Park Avenue, recently excerpted by *The New York Times,* caused a ruckus.

It focused on a small group of uberprivileged, educated Manhattan women who get "wife bonuses" from their conspicuously powerful husbands for staying lithe, keeping the domestic staff in good order, and rearing high-achieving children—*think Pretty Woman,* except Julia Roberts has a law degree she doesn't use.

So we asked ourselves: Is this an enviable position, one we'd secretly covet?

The other question we asked was this: What's a "marriage bonus"? Is that a joke? Do you serve at your spouse's pleasure, is it a pay-per-lap-dance thing, or is it a "go ahead, toots, buy yourself a bathrobe" deal?

The author, "Wednesday" Martin (her real name is Wendy, but I guess she liked *The Addams Family*), snagged our attention with money and sex but kept it by sounding scholarly. Using the language of a disinterested observer, for example, when discussing her neighbors on the Upper East Side Martin announces: "It didn't take long for me to realize that my background in anthropology might help me figure it all out, and that this elite tribe and its practices made for a fascinating story."

Don't you always love it when the folks next door reach that conclusion?

Martin appeared to study the world through the lens of academic discourse. Sprinkling references to the Agta women of the Philippines and !Kung women of Africa next to stories of spin classes and playdates made her sound distant, erudite, and objective.

Martin presented the Upper East Side's tribe's transactional marriages in such a way that my friend Alan Hochbaum calls them tennis relationships because "love means nothing."

The commodification of children makes Lisa, a New York business writer, wonder, "How many of them were conceived ASAP to seal such marriage mergers?"

Christopher P. Larsen, a stay-at-home dad, suggests that these spouses have gone from being "friends with benefits" to "employees without benefits"—except for the husbandly handouts—and that maybe the subjection is what "turns these guys on."

Fifty shades of green, anyone?

But a long interview with Martin in the *New York Post* followed on the heels of the piece in the *Times* and tripped her up.

Martin confessed she was a "total buy-in" to the life she studied. "Something about these arrogant women, who pushed and crowded me like I didn't exist, made me want a beautiful, expensive bag."

Really? It made me want to join a union.

Martin felt a Hermès Birkin, a pocketbook that sells for up to $150,000, would help her self-esteem. So her financier husband bought her one. Martin felt better.

Look, for $150K you can hire a college graduate to carry your stuff for two years. You wouldn't need a purse.

This was when I stopped taking Martin seriously. It was as if Jane Goodall had morphed into Mildred Pierce's daughter.

The interview with a Queen Bee Wannabe who whined for a purse clashed with the voice of authority making opprobrious pronouncements about "those women."

Martin says she "went native" (a remarkably insulting term). Now living across town surrounded by women with "post-menopausal gray hair" who don't "care about the last ten pounds," the author misses the "immaculate and conservative and clean" tribe she left a good twelve, maybe fifteen, minutes away.

Martin's book does not reflect the lives of most women in Manhattan any more than *Mob Wives* illustrates the lives of most women on Staten Island.

A college friend who loves living on the Upper East Side declares Martin's landscape unrecognizable. "I've never met one of the creatures described in the *Primates* book," says Elizabeth Kadin. "Guess going to work, using public transportation, and shopping at Ann Taylor LOFT keeps me insulated from them."

Others are less generous. "I hope the women she infiltrated and betrayed and whose values she seems to share eat her for lunch," wrote my friend Margaret, who then added: "However, they probably don't eat lunch."

Wednesday Martin would probably remind them that, especially if they don't care about those last ten pounds, they could always eat cake.

6

Women's Bodies—from an Amusement Park to a Terrarium

From age sixteen to age twenty, a woman's body is a temple. From twenty-one to forty-five, it's an amusement park. From forty-five on, it's a terrarium.

I know this because every morning I now take a capsule with 4.6 billion strains of supposedly beneficial flora to help establish the equilibrium in my digestive tract. There are only 7 billion people on the planet. Every morning I'm swallowing half my own universe.

And I'm not the only one. Every person I meet who is even in the least bit neurotic about his or her—it's usually her—intestinal issues takes some version of a probiotic. I didn't know what a probiotic was until a year ago, but now it's emerged, right alongside philosophy, politics, and the latest international security breach, as a central topic of discussion.

I take a pill, and I have no idea what's in it. I've tried to learn; I read the small print. But I don't get the explanation. It doesn't help that the people explaining it are usually the same ones who have attempted to explain how derivatives function in economic terms. My role is to stand in front of them as they deliver earnest and passionate speeches until my eyes glaze over and I start to wobble.

Indeed, I believe some of the same people who once sold derivatives are now selling probiotics, but it just could be that they have similar facial expressions and that, at some point, I'm expected to make use of a checkbook.

Anyway, I take this pill every morning before my first sip of decaf. I'm not allowed to have caffeine anymore because it's not good for me, whereas becoming a host to microorganisms is something to celebrate. For all I know, I'm ingesting the very stuff I scrape off the tiles in my shower stall. Yet I do it because I'm convinced it's suddenly imperative I assist the side of righteousness in the struggle taking place in my colon where, apparently, ignorant armies clash by night.

The word on Wellness Street is that our mental, physical, and spiritual hygiene hinges on the effective landscaping of our tummies. As if there's a little gardener in there, some guy with a weed whacker and a couple of bags of bulbs.

Do we find this odd? Nope. We say, "Oh, good! At last I know what's been bugging me all these years!" And then we buy specially formulated yogurt advertised by a well-known actress who looks like a fun, *regular* person. With the emphasis on "regular."

Human beings are always searching for some part of our body to blame. In the fifteenth century, you could go to a healer who used leeches, holy water, and spiders to cure you. If the patient lived, he gave the healer a pound of goat meat; if he died, the healer was burnt to death as a witch. This is why, even today, doctors prefer malpractice insurance to its alternatives.

In our lifetimes, the quick fixes have changed rapidly. Once upon a time it was iron we all lacked; people took Geritol (remember the ad saying: "My wife—I think I'll keep her"?). Then it was water. Suddenly everybody in America was discovering water like it was a miracle beverage, not like you could get it from a hydrant. Then all of a sudden it was vitamin D that was going to save us.

Now it's internal shrubbery.

And that's why women are taking capsules filled with forests and have turned into a version of Botanical Gardens, except in heels. Sensible heels, mind you, because everything in life is about balance.

We're crossing the border where human beings and plant life meet. We're hybrids. We're like the pod people in those bad science-fiction movies except we're not trying to escape; this time we're running down the street chasing the six-foot string bean so that we can ask for its help with our colitis. The string bean is attempting to evade our grasp because we're too needy and emotionally dependent on it. Talk about scary.

Maybe we should go back to thinking about our bodies as temples. There could be offerings. I'd like pepperoni and extra cheese on mine.

7

Let the Good Times In

We all enter this world crying. Laughter is something we have to learn.

We learn to laugh through contact with somebody else who's doing it, which, unless you're a twin, is yet another difference from the whole "being born" business.

And although it is possible to laugh alone, like so many other things, it's a lot more fun to do it with others. I'm thinking, of course, of miniature golf.

My journalist friend Gene Weingarten, of *The Washington Post*, says the very moment we learn to laugh depends on having somebody else there. He believes it all comes down to peekaboo. (Yes, like so many other things.)

Weingarten argues that "peekaboo tickles before tickling tickles" and the experience of humor goes back to the moment when a baby watches somebody cover her face with her hands and then yell "peekaboo!" in glee as she removes them. That irrepressible combination of surprise-plus-continuity is at the heart of it, says Weingarten.

We adore being a little bit shocked, but we also immediately want to see that our shock is just silly. We want to be reminded, by the release of laughter, that what we love has not actually disappeared.

Psychologists refer to this as "object permanence." Perhaps you've referred to it in less clinical terms if, as I have, you have begun what turned into a marathon session of peekaboo with a tyke who has been affected by too much excitement, sugar, or double-espresso shots. Kids will play peekaboo until the cows come home, or until it simply smells as if they did.

Our appetite for that kind of fun dwindles as we grow up. It is replaced by the mind-numbing drudgery of life. After all, there's kindergarten with its endless crayoning, crayoning, and crayoning. And school? With the horror of, well, learning? And sitting? And snacking before learning again? No wonder we lose our mirth.

A sense of humor is not hardwired into our systems once we get past the peekaboo stage; if you've ever commuted to work by bus you know this for a fact. But a sense of humor can be developed as can another talent or skill set. Like carrying a tune or picking up the check, however, some people never master the art.

Some folks don't realize that there is no such thing as an ordinary life.

They believe themselves to have cornered the market on misery, frustration, and disappointment. They tell you about their unhappy childhoods and dysfunctional families as if they were the only ones ever to have been ritually humiliated, even before *America's Funniest Home Videos* went global. They complain about their parents, kids, jobs, or neighbors to the point where their tales of woe are, like certain exotic foods, hard to swallow.

But bad times, we must remember, are inevitable: we all face death: we all face suffering: we all face the prospect of another season of *Dance Moms*. You have two alternatives: you can crack up or you can crack a smile.

Unlike bad times, however, good times aren't bullies that

break down the doors and barge in. Joy and pleasure are, instead, excellent guests and, as such, they wait for an invitation. You have to open the door to life's best moments; you have to invite them in and welcome them when they arrive.

To be honest, I've always found that it's best to make a big fuss when good times appear at the threshold. You want them to feel absolutely at home. You wouldn't want them to feel that, while you're happy enough to see them, you were expecting a little more razzle-dazzle. They might not come again. They depend on genuine hospitality. You wouldn't want them to think they'd arrived too late, or were deemed insignificant, or were weighed and found wanting.

Survival, or making survival worth the bother, depends on seeking joy, uncovering and discovering humor, and, in one of life's great ironies, carefully nurturing a sense of the absurd.

Remembering to laugh is as essential as learning how to peek-aboo in the first place. It can't make the darkness go away, but it does admit the light.

8

Bring Your Sense of Humor . . . and Nineteen More Rules to Live By

1. Bring your sense of humor with you at all times. Bring your friends with a sense of humor. If their friends have a sense of humor, invite them, too. Remember this when going to hospitals, weight-loss centers, and funerals, as well as when going to work, coming home, waking up, and going to sleep.

2. If it's worth crying over, it's probably worth laughing at. Cultivate a sense of perspective that permits you to see the wider and longer view of the situation; this will help you realize that although your situation is upsetting, it might also one day become a terrific story.

3. Other people don't care what you're wearing.

4. Don't be a sissy. This is especially important if you are a woman. Girls can be sissies, but behaving like a simpering, whining, fretful coward as an adult is unacceptable no matter what your gender happens to be. If you are anxious, scared, and feeling powerless, you don't need to change your behavior; you need to change your life.

5. Don't lie. Cheat the devil and tell the truth.

6. There is one exception to the rule above: never say a baby looks like a sausage wearing a hat. The parents will not forgive you. This is a situation in which telling the truth is not wholly necessary. If it's not possible to tell the whole truth for fear of causing undue pain, just say the baby looks "happy."

7. Never use the passive voice. Do not say, "It will get done." Say, "I'll do it," and then offer a solid, unwavering deadline. Always make your deadline.

8. The pinnacle is always slippery; no peak is safe. Only plateaus offer a place to rest. Are you ready to stay on a plateau or are you climbing? Decide and pack your bags accordingly.

9. As we age, love changes. As a youth, you fall for an unattainable ideal. When you're more mature, you fall in love with a person: "Sure, he has only one eye in the middle of his forehead," you'll rationalize, "but he never forgets my birthday."

10. Power is the ability to persuade stupid people to do intelligent things and intelligent people to do stupid things. This is why power is dangerous.

11. Sherlock Holmes said, "Work is the best antidote to sorrow, my dear Watson." Listen to Mr. Holmes.

12. Everybody wants a shortcut to love, prosperity, and weight loss, although not necessarily in that order. Apart from being born into an adoring family, getting good genes, and inheriting the mineral rights, however, there are no shortcuts. The rest of us have to work at it.

13. Help the dramatically self-pitying to understand that they are not, by definition, sympathetic or interesting. Encourage them to address topics other than themselves.

14. Be kind, not nice. Kindness is both intentional and meaningful. Acts of kindness require generosity, emotional and otherwise. Perfunctory and superficial niceness is, too often, mere window dressing.

15. Only poor workers blame their tools. It's not the fault of the computer, the school, the train, the government, or poor cell phone reception. Take responsibility.

16. You know how sometimes you don't think you're asleep— you're half-listening to a conversation or the television—only to discover you were unconscious? One part of your head would swear it's awake, but when you actually snap out of it you realize you were wholly elsewhere? Sometimes that happens in life. Sometimes the only way you know you're truly in love, in the entirely wrong profession, being a moron at parties, or a great poet is when you snap out of it.

17. You can always stop what you're doing.

18. Either you should be doing something useful or you should be playing. You should not be thinking about playing while at work or thinking about work when you're out having fun. Compartmentalizing your life is not inevitably a bad thing. It's easy to

waste pleasure by feeling guilty and waste potentially effective time by feeling resentful.

19. Be aware that a safety net, if pulled too tight, easily turns into a noose. Don't trade independence for security without being aware of the consequences.

20. Someday you will die. Until then, you should do everything possible to enjoy life.

9

Achievement Dysmorphia

If you want to get into an argument with a woman, compliment her.

Say she did an excellent job on her project, on her assignment, or with her fund-raiser and then watch what happens. Whether you're applauding her for the skillful handling of a complex situation or cheering her for the quicksilver nature of her problem solving, she will nod, offer a tight-lipped smile, and proceed to explain, in earnest, why you're wrong.

"My team did everything." "If only I had another week!" "Are you kidding? I'm nowhere near my expectations."

She'll keep talking, too, apologizing and offering details. Men back away slowly, scratching their heads and swearing never to say another word. Other women murmur soothing noises because we understand.

I often offer soothing noises. For three years, a close friend has been writing a novel. Her publisher sent an e-mail, which included the glorious phrase: "It's terrific. Consider the book accepted," as well as suggestions for a few changes for the final chapter. She forwarded me his note. I focused on "terrific" and "accepted," but she focused on his edits as evidence that she was not, and probably never would be, good enough. She feels lightweight, amateurish, and as if she's been caught pilfering rather than earning her success.

She suffers from what I call achievement dysmorphia, or the sense of disconnection women experience when our manifest accomplishments and our sense of unworthiness don't line up. It isn't quite the imposter syndrome—it's not about faking a persona, but instead it's about a reluctance to accept victory and enjoy even an earned sense of triumph.

Cue Rosemary Clooney singing "I Enjoy Being a Girl."

Over the years, we've learned about body dysmorphia, a recurrent, relentless dissatisfaction so profound it compels a woman to diet, exercise, or scrub her face compulsively because she can't stand her appearance.

(Such behavior is not hardwired, either; female gerbils do not spend hours wondering whether they've spent enough time on the treadmill that day. They do not search under the wood chips for tiny foundation garments if they feel some fat under their fur.)

Cultural conditioning causes us to undermine ourselves ritually and we accept the self-sabotage as if we were born to it.

Actually, we're almost but not quite born to it: if you see a very little girl look into a mirror, you'll probably see her smile. But the older she gets, the more that smile is tinged with chagrin. By the time she's grown into her adult body, she's probably dissatisfied with it.

This profound sense of discomfort inside one's own skin is so widely accepted as part of women's lives that huge corporations such as Unilever, owners of Dove products, capitalize on it. Dove now has a "Self-Esteem Toolkit" as part of its website to help girls "embrace their unique beauty."

Great, right? Except Unilever also owns AXE products marketed to young men. Are young men encouraged by AXE to discover the unique beauty in every individual? Let's see. The AXE website declares: "Girls are getting hotter! Keep your cool with new AXE." Hmmm.

This tells us that women are identified first by their beauty—and belief in their beauty is worn away long before they are old enough to understand that it would be better for them to build their identities on their strengths, skills, and talents. But after all, vanity in girls is encouraged; pride is discouraged. If this were not the case, there would be ego moisturizers alongside the ones for your face.

The world persists in categorizing women as either pretty or smart, nice or ambitious, and feminine or feminist even though, if you're civilized enough to sleep lying down and not standing on all fours, you already know these divisions are artificial. They only exist because some guy, a long time ago, decided: "Hey, if we don't start compartmentalizing women, they'll be all *over* the place!"

And now women are all over the place, or soon will be.

It's taken a few thousand years, but we're on it.

10

Occupy Vogue

I am the 99 percent: I am not part of the 1 percent of American women whom designers consider when they pull together an outfit made from two Band-Aids and some chain-link fence, call it evening wear, and sell it for $9,867 before tax.

Like most American women, I am a size 14. I am not a size 4, a size 0, or a size Sub-Zero. A Sub-Zero, for me, is a kind of refrigerator. Although that hints at the reason my dress size isn't exactly in single digits, it also illustrates one of the real issues facing women: our time is misspent, our frustrations are fueled, and our energies are depleted by the hours we spend every week searching for one lousy garment we can wear on those occasions when we give a damn how we look.

Those running the country—the 1 percent we hear so much about—who want to jump-start the economy and get our nation's workplaces humming again might want to listen to this suggestion: Make clothes that every woman, regardless of her economic status, weight, or height, will look good in. Permit us to spend whatever we can on a piece of attire that makes us look and feel good and you'll make a million bucks a day without breaking a sweat.

Maybe we could also get rid of overseas sweatshops. If clothes were made in America again, we could find outfits to fit our grain-fed American bodies. That way, we can stop relying on wee French models or small women from other exotic places such as, say, the planet Naboo.

You can't convince me that women from anywhere on this earth are small enough to fit into what are laughingly called sample sizes. Only in Paris or in other galaxies far, far away is it physically possible for any life-form to exist without possessing a rump.

What does it say about our culture when women are encouraged to bare our bodies but keep everything else—our ambitions, our hourly wages, and whether or not we are fans of *The Good Wife*—secret? After all, Freud in *Three Essays on the Theory of Sexuality* argued: "The progressive concealment of the body, which goes along with civilization, keeps sexual curiosity awake." Maybe that's why so many guys are falling asleep at the wheel, or the stick shift.

It's the whole brain that's tickled by curiosity and excited by a potential partner—sex is not just a plate of wings. There's more to the whole business than thighs and hot sauce.

Fashion designers don't understand this. If you look at Victoria's Secret, it's like the owners of Perdue chicken: they focus exclusively on breasts, with maybe a few feathers thrown in. And nobody really likes the feathers.

But what else can we expect, really? When a media focused on the wealthy, the powerful, the thin, the cosseted, and the carefully sinewed creates our idea of "the world," how do we reconcile our ordinary lives with those in *People* magazine? If I'm standing in line at the grocery store looking at the issue with red-carpet celebrities, what I'm thinking is: "If those are people, what am I?"

The rest of us, wearing six shades of mismatched black, including a cowl-neck sweater we liked in college, don't feel entirely human. We're getting tired of it.

The 1 percent of corporate magnates who run this country are throwing both erotic and economic health into a state of distress by not paying attention to what real people, particularly real women, need.

We need fair wages (and since we're on the topic, that means women earning 100 percent of what men earn). We need a system in which even those without economic clout have a strong political voice. We need workplace policies that reflect the lives of working people, with evidence that those who make and maintain the rules know that living, breathing human beings are affected by these conditions.

I'd say it's time for women to make a stand. And it's far, far easier to make a stand when you're wearing comfortable shoes. Mine are size 7½ W, $39.99, purchased four years ago from T.J.Maxx, and working just fine.

11

Loud Women Talking

Ever notice how women get noisy as we age? Ever notice how the quiet, deferential, focused good girl hits a certain point and morphs into a combination of Betty White, Bette Midler, and Bette Davis?

That's because when women start to feel invisible we decide to become audible.

Over thirty-eight, forty, fifty—every woman comes to the stage when she ceases to be the ingénue, but it happens to us at different ages—we start making trouble: talking back and speaking up without waiting for anybody else's cue.

Increasingly political, assertive, articulate, and outspoken as we age, many of us become, paradoxically, the girls we once were: wild, hearty, courageous, and playful.

I believe this happens once you start calling us ma'am and we stop crying about it. We all remember our first "ma'am" moment. Initially it's a shock to realize we've moved from "darlin'" to "ma'am"—and few women want to put that experience on their "best day ever" list.

Yet slipping off feminine propriety is like stripping out of a too-tight dress. And kicking off the goody-two-shoes pretense is like sending a pair of high heels flying across the room after a long day.

The big changes in women's lives are not menopause or the end of child rearing or any other Margaret Mead anthropological slide show; the biggest thing that happens to any woman is when she stops being the ingénue.

When she hears herself addressed as "ma'am," there's a kind of emotional Doppler effect: her identity as the youngest and most sparkling woman around rushes past her.

All she can hear of the professional and personal praise she once sought or of the wolf whistles—sought or shunned—is the sound of silence. And neither Simon nor Garfunkel is singing.

In that silence she finds her own voice and she learns how to use it.

We'll tell you the truth and we won't sugarcoat it; we'll laugh only when your stories are funny; we'll argue until the sun goes down or comes up again without batting an eye—let alone fluttering an eyelash in a flirtatious attempt to get you to settle down.

We don't want to settle down anymore; we've been settled, like some western township, and now we want to kick up the dust and tear down the fences. Not only won't we settle down; we also won't settle for less than what we've always wanted: a good time and a fair fight.

No, this is not an advertisement for menopause or a polemic against a fully realized, string-bikini-wearing youth; every phase of life has its delicious moments. And I've always believed that the one unforgivable sin was to wish your life away by trying to hurry through it. When my hair was long and my attention span was short, I was tickled pink to be ogled. Now I am tickled pink to be heard, especially because it's tough to be ogled and listened to at the same time. Frankly, the whole ogling thing gets old faster than cheap panty hose.

You've probably noticed that you can hear women over forty even when you aren't looking. Not that we give up on looking good. For proof of that, just glance at advertising foldouts in women's magazines declaring how forty is the new thirty, sixty is the new forty, and death is the new life in order to get us to keep buying products made from (but more expensive than) caviar and precious metals. (I'm not even kidding: there are now skin products supposedly created with 24-karat gold extract. I guess if financial times got really tough, you could always pawn your own head.)

What you'll hear less of, however, are apologies, pleas for favors, and requests for permission. Grown-up women understand that what we need is a welcoming place to be exactly and unapologetically who we are. Like every human being, we need friends, significant work, and somebody who wants to make sure we get home OK. But let's not kid ourselves: good insurance, excellent food, and great sex are also important and not necessarily in that order.

You only live once, but if you do it right, once is enough. You just have to live it up.

12

Growing Old Gaudily

I've lived my life with enthusiasm, courage, raucousness, and passion. Why on earth would I want to grow old gracefully?

Why would I want to be Whistler's mother when my whole life who I've wanted to be is Mae West?

Let's face it: it's about as likely that I'll become calm, serene, and dignified as I age as it was that I'd be prim, proper, and sweet in my youth.

Those were always lovely fantasies—for somebody else. But like charming dresses that would never flatter me, I don't fit into these patterns. They weren't designed with me in mind. No matter how I try to tailor them or hold my breath long enough to slip them on, I know they'd be confining, inappropriate, and impossible to carry off.

But "growing old gracefully" is one of those phrases we've heard so often that we've internalized the concept without examining it. I've decided that as I age, rather than becoming contemplative and introspective, I want to become more disruptive, seditious, and boisterous instead.

Over forty, you get louder. Over fifty, you're just loud.

Not only am I not going gentle into that good night; I am also not going gracefully into that late afternoon. I intend to go as gentle as a mastodon stuck in a tar pit.

I want to be one of those women who brandish a cane. I come from a family of people with bad knees, so that particular accessory is probably in my future. But I don't plan to "carry," "rely upon," or "make occasional use" of a cane, but to brandish it. The two things a person can brandish are canes and swords and I'm unlikely to model myself after either Xena, the Warrior Princess, or Joan of Arc at this stage (although anything is possible). Cane it is.

I might also start carrying a flask. It might contain gin; it might contain Ensure. What it contains is beside the point: what matters is that I will be able to whip out a flask.

I might also begin to dispense some of my possessions to the young under my care. This will happen in those instances where I can now afford to purchase higher-quality goods. "Please take this handmade quilt. Grandma's gonna get some sheets from Frette."

After fifty, you can begin to distinguish what actually makes you happy from what you've always done to please others. Being able to define that difference is an accomplishment. It's one of those areas of expertise that takes at least 10,000 hours to learn.

After a certain age, you finally become the indisputable authority on the subject of yourself.

It's absurd to think that you're then supposed to spend all your time sitting quietly while people tell you dull stories about their kids (whom you don't know), their dogs (who have a limited range of talents, although often cuter and less self-involved than their kids), or their gallbladder surgery (more engaging than either offspring or pets).

Is it simply a lack of imagination that makes us view any time after middle age as a time of life when people are mostly worried about what will get stuck in their trachea? Or is it because we're still bound by weirdly constructed and entirely arbitrary definitions telling us how people are supposed to act at a certain age?

When I was a girl, I was told I wasn't supposed to be energetic, ambitious, or competitive. I was told I wasn't supposed to be fierce, seditious, or demanding. I didn't listen then; why would I listen now, when I'm being told essentially the same thing—a version of "Sit down and be quiet"?

It's easy to say that what I really want for my eightieth birthday is to be surrounded by loved ones and to have my health, but what I truly believe I'll want on my eightieth birthday is a leased Ferrari and a month at the Waldorf. If I'm lucky, I have a little time to make plans.

On his deathbed, my father preferred prosecco sipped from a straw to chicken soup; he was a good role model.

Better to be a legend first—and then craft a legacy.

13

Turn It Up; I'm Dancing

Just as "one size fits all" is an incomplete sentence, so is describing people as "older:" Even in terms of sentence construction, it sidesteps the real question. Older than what? Older than whom? Older than fashion models? My cat is older than many fashion models. I won't even discuss the fact that she also weighs more.

As a nation, we have become so fearful of using the word "old" that we'll do anything to dance around it. We'll dance around the definition of "old" while the band plays on—and the band is playing oldies. The band is playing Creedence Clearwater Revival; the band is playing The Doors; the band is playing Joni Mitchell.

I'm reconfiguring my steps because I'm celebrating my birthday this week. I have the privilege of turning fifty-eight. I see birthdays as a reward for having shown up 365 days in a row. It's like getting a badge for attendance.

Jokes about weight aside, I'm relieved to be twice the woman I used to be. I wouldn't be twenty-nine again for money. Half a lifetime ago I was frantically finishing my dissertation, applying for jobs, growing exponentially unhappy in my first marriage, living in a dark basement apartment, and uncertain about whether I'd ever pay off my student loans.

Age twenty-nine, especially for a woman, has been long regarded as one of those Magic 8 Ball numbers wherein you can register your destiny. The age still holds a sort of uncanny shimmer for my students, who believe that what they are at twenty-nine is what they will be forever.

I saw it as the age where I was meant to shed my girlhood entirely, the way rocket ships jettison the fancy, complicated apparatus that launches the essential craft into space, leaving the encapsulated version to make the voyage, because it would go farther and, with luck, survive longer.

Morphing from the ingénue to the adult, I realized that you're always brand-new at whatever stage of life you enter.

Only very specific kinds of expertise are transferable. If you've spent every moment of your youth the way you'd spend every coin in your pocket, then you've got a wealth of experience upon which to build. If you mostly watched reruns, tried on blouses, and waited for stuff to come out of the microwave, you might feel a little empty-handed.

You might have been great at being twenty or thirty, but that doesn't mean you'll necessarily be great at being forty or fifty.

If we're all going to be old dogs, we'd better be willing to learn some new tricks. The fun part is this: there are also some new treats.

(The only folks who seem willing to talk about these treats, however, are Dr. Ruth and the AARP. Those of us who are enjoying the third act of our lives should be more generous about letting other people know that it's not just one bowl of oatmeal after the other.)

I've also realized that, at fifty-eight, I am in my third act. When listening to Julianne Moore's acceptance speech at the Golden Globe Awards, I was struck by her saying, "When Lisa Genova wrote this book, she told me that no one wanted to make it into a movie because no one wanted to see a movie about a middle-aged woman."

As I was sitting there on Sunday night in my pajamas in front of the television with my fashion model cat on my lap, it occurred to me that no longer do I come under the aegis of being middle-aged. Julianne Moore might be middle-aged—I could see her making it to 108—but the odds of my making it to 116, given my fondness for disco fries, are slim to none.

For me intermission has passed and we've all been reseated. I wouldn't say the lights are being dimmed quite yet, but I am starting to look covetously at those eyeglasses I once ridiculed—the ones with the tiny LED lights built into the frames.

But if you believe that your best years are behind you, you've guaranteed they are; I'm going to dance into that good night, with the oldies turned up loud.

14

When Faith's Needed, I Don't Have a Prayer

I admire people of faith but am made nervous by those who live in a spiritually gated community.

God knows I'm not religious, but I consider it a privilege to know people who are—just as I am honored to know people who are brilliant mathematicians even though I personally still count on my fingers.

Good folks have offered to instruct me in both areas of study. Yet despite suspecting my life (not to mention my afterlife) might be way better for it, I thank them and decline.

But I'm not too proud to ask for their help: when, for example, death and taxes find me at their doors.

Here's my deal with religion: I'm a believer in the power of other people's faith. I do not share their faiths, but I have belief in their enviable belief that someone (often with a capital *S*), some entity, somewhere is looking out for us.

So entirely am I willing to throw my lot in with theirs, in fact, that I have no shame in asking a friend to say a prayer for me—or even one of my loved ones—when necessary. I feel like their prayers have an express route and a tracking number whereas my own efforts would wind up in the dead letter office.

If I'm asked to help, I tell people I can offer them a good thought, a hug, meat loaf, a book, or pudding: I'm not up to saying a prayer because I wouldn't know what to do anymore. The old ones I repeat so entirely by rote they sound like jump-rope rhymes. The new ones, the ones I try to make up from the heart, sound overwrought, pretentious, and absurd in equal measure.

Trust me when I say I'm better at meat loaf; my cooking is more sincere. The ingredients are fresher, less adulterated, and more worthy.

It's not that my family didn't try. I was raised a Roman Catholic, but it was the kind of domesticated Catholicism that focused mostly on the length of your skirt rather than, say, the depth of your penitential observance.

Certainly, I identified as a Catholic. I was helped by the fact that the years of my childhood were a big time for nuns: There was *The Singing Nun* (complete with Grammy-winning single), there was Rosalind Russell playing a nun in a successful movie, *The Trouble with Angels* (directed by Ida Lupino, no less), and there was *The Flying Nun* (complete with bubble-gum cards) starring Sally Field.

And although I didn't go to Catholic school, because it was too expensive, I knew several nuns, since we lived right near a church. Many of them would stop by to chat with my aunts. This was a big deal. At least one of my aunts had attempted to join an order but couldn't make it, so I suspect there was a sense of wistfulness behind her friendliness. (There was also a little resentment; I remember her joking, "Why are they called nuns? None of this, none of that.")

Yet my background in religious instruction was no more effective than my training in arithmetic. Most of my serious personal religious instruction came from reading leaflets. There were dozens of them, new ones every month, covering everything from "Is It Lust or Love?" and "The Catholic Girl's Guide to Teen Life" to

"Impure Thoughts: Danger Zone!"—all available for a dime's donation. These were, in effect, CliffsNotes for the soul. They summed up, dumbed down, and misled; they inoculated me against having to deal with genuine moral questions by diverting me with the difference between "petting" and "heavy petting."

I stopped going to church at sixteen, when my mother died.

She'd been a devout Catholic, dying with the rosary wrapped woven between her fingers, but wanted to be cremated. Our parish disapproved and refused to grant her a funeral mass. A family friend who happened to be a priest said prayers, but he did it, not as a representative of the church, but as a personal favor.

Is it a surprise, then, that since that time I've learned to count on the faith of favors, offered with love and given freely? Kindness is a convincing prayer.

PART 2

Sex Is Not the Answer.

"Sex?" Is the Question

15

The Female Orgasm, In Her Own Words,
Explains How She Is Not Elusive

Let me introduce myself. You probably weren't expecting me—
so few do—and yet since I've been so often on your tongue, I
thought I'd just pop in.

I'm neither elusive nor a mystery once you get to know me—
and I certainly hope you will. I'm not mythological, darling. I'm
not like a ghost or like Bigfoot. I actually do exist.

When can you expect me? Are you asking me to make an appointment? It doesn't work that way. I like a good time. When I
know people are relaxing, having intimate conversations, really
enjoying themselves both cheerfully and intensely, you'll find
that I'm drawn to the moment.

Contrary to what you might have been told, I don't need a big
party, a lot of decorations, too much to drink, or a whole lot of fuss;
I don't need a red carpet, so to speak, because I carry my own with
me, all rolled up and tucked into place. I don't need a big limo,
either, or a Hummer. If I need to, I can walk and get to where I'm
going.

Despite what you may have heard from someone who's never
known me personally, I'm not all about making a scene. You might
have seen me and not recognized me. There are times I hardly

know myself, to be honest. There are times I'm all about shouting my name out loud and there are times I'm snuggled under a sigh.

If something odd is going on, or I'm distracted by a tense situation or something unfamiliar—a deadline, a new place, a new face, the sound of a car alarm or a baby's cry—try as I might to show up, there are times I can't make it. I'm not good under pressure. Sometimes I'm best when I'm alone.

My pet peeve? Impersonators. Those clowns who pretend to be me. When I see them caricature my genuine passion and make fools out of themselves doing bizarre imitations of what they think I'd be like under those weird circumstances—cameras, banks of light, fifteen people in a hot tub, and a G-string made out of dental floss—I want to call a good lawyer and sue.

But I have too much else to do and too many other places to be to worry about the fakes and the phonies. I just feel sorry for those people who fall for the bad acting and confuse a terrible performance by a second-rate wannabe for the real thing.

And, like anybody who gets more than her fair share of gossip and comment, I'm always secretly fascinated to read what others say about me: where I come from, how I've changed over the years, who needs me, who wants me, whether I'm just a sidekick or the leading lady, whether—ultimately—I really matter at all. Scientists say I don't count; glossy magazines say it's all about the glad-handing. Usually I just laugh, but I thought it might just be time you heard it from me directly.

So let me leave you with one thought: Darling, the very last thing I am is elusive. All the girls know me—or have known me at some point. If I'm elusive or mysterious to you, kiddo, maybe you're not doing something right.

16

Rules on Love, Laughter, and Using Your Words

We hold these sexual truths to be self-evident:

1. As George Bernard Shaw advised, it is not always a good idea to treat others as you would like to be treated, since their taste might differ from yours. If, for example, your partner likes a whisper-soft and gentle fluttering of the fingertips, do *not* use your hands in a way that suggests you're churning butter or flattening pizza dough. But if your mate is ticklish, the *least* soothing touch might be a gentle one—it can replace his or her erotic mood with a supremely annoyed one. You need to consider not what you *think* your partner wants, but what he or she *actually* wants.

2. Speaking of wants, talk, using grown-up words, about what you actually want. This might be a conversation to have before you begin anything physical—maybe several hours or several days before you begin acting on those wants. (Rarely is it wisest to initiate such discourse in the middle of the main course.) What's remarkable and yet totally common is the shyness even sexually active couples have about putting into words what they like and don't like. You'd think long-term partners would be able to say,

"Let's use position seventeen, with side orders of twelve and nine," but often they just can't. If anything, long-term partners grow to be *increasingly* shy about changes in their sexual tastes, instead passively permitting the menu to remain the same. The courage to *speak* about sex instead of simply *having* sex is crucial.

3. Laughing together is an underestimated aphrodisiac. The eye contact, the sense of connection, the warmth, and physical relaxation of a shared funny moment can lead to later moments of heat. I'm always surprised when heroes in romantic movies kiss the heroines when the ladies are weeping; it seems far more likely that a deep, genuine *laugh* would end in kisses than bursting into tears—not to mention being more fun.

4. You can't be dignified *and* be sexy. Be playful. Be indulgent. Be patient. Be extravagant. Be silly. But give up any and all attempts to be dignified. Remember, even Queen Victoria had nine children; at times, even *she* must have been . . . amused.

5. But don't ignore hygiene just because you've been together before or you've been together forever. Do I need to say more? Make an effort! Take three minutes and clean yourself off and up and under and in-between. If you don't think it's worth even that much work, you may need to rethink your choices.

6. Sex should not be a competition. You don't "win" by having an orgasm. You most certainly won't help your partner "win" by employing the kind of focused diligence typically used by deputies to serve subpoenas. If you're trying to feel a sense of total immersion in the moment, then turning an act of intimacy into a contest complete with grand slams, receivers, doubles, servers, and break

points, is probably not your best choice. Focus instead on the much more daring score of "love."

7. Turn off all electronic devices. Or, for heaven's sake, at least put them on vibrate. . . .

17

Define That Feeling

You're an average-aged (too old for work–study, too young for cremation) person in a committed relationship, but one day you suddenly discover you've got a crush on somebody. You're infatuated by a coworker, a neighbor, or even—why now?—an old friend. Life gets a little fizzy and a little fuzzy. You're checking electronic devices for cute text messages and searching for nuances in e-mails. You discover flirtatious implications whether or not they're actually there; that's the foolish part.

Like the flu or a bout of colitis, the best thing to do is to sit tight and hope it passes quickly, before too many people notice and before anybody else is infected.

What you are, of course, is infatuated. The word "infatuated" is derived from the Latin "fatuus," meaning "foolish," or, as some linguists argue, "too heavy in the thigh area for an assignation."

You didn't think people got crushes at this age? Good luck. I have a ninety-one-year-old friend who is worried that her eighty-eight-year-old husband is having an emotional affair with a younger woman in their congregation. The femme fatale in question is eighty-five, making the "fatale" part of the phrase a little more literal than usual. Yet my friend is as indignant and jealous as a teenager. "That one is wooing him with cooked meats," she snarls. "She's part of the Brisket Brigade. I don't care; I'm going to out-last her. Plus I still have better legs."

Here's what another friend wrote and gave me permission to repeat:

Am I not too old for all of this? Am I not too wise and exper-ienced to wait to hear from a man? I know better; I'm accus-tomed to my own self-deceptions and sleights of hand. I should be able to say, "Okay, this is **THAT** feeling. I KNOW **THAT** feeling and it doesn't do me any good. The dry mouth, dry enough to make my lipstick stick to my teeth, is no good. The fast heartbeat, the skin that is so thin it tingles, the ears waiting for some sound, some signal of reassurance—it's all **THAT** feeling."

I can see it, I can name it, and now I have to learn to drive it away with sticks or smoke or weapons, anything, because it needs to be driven out like an infection or the barbarian at the gate. Except—and this is the tricky part—maybe the attraction *is* the barbarian at the gate—the force of chaos outside the walls. Maybe that's why we call emotions floods and arguments storms and sudden infatuations *coups de foudre*.

I thought I was out of the game altogether. I thought I'd put my costumes in a trunk and put the trunks into the cellar—not even putting them under the bed, not even hedging my bets that I might need to get at them quick and find them in a hurry or in the dark. I'd relaxed into the belief that I could put the tools of that trade away and let them rust. But I was kidding myself in the most ridiculous of ways—I was treating myself like a child, saying, "No, you mustn't," and then slapping my own hand away when I tried to sneak desire into the room, as if I could clamp down and cauterize part of myself.

I want to dance. I don't want to stand in one place and tap my feet to a rhythm I can hardly hear but can't ignore. Out there is a party with music I know. But I'm worried I'd slip and trip and fall and lose more than my slipper. I'm worried I'll risk what little dignity I have. I fear no good will come of it. And yet . . . I'm putting my dancing shoes on. I know the words. I remember the rhythm. And maybe I don't need "good" to come of it. Maybe what I need a little bit of is exactly the opposite of "good."

So there you are, like my friend, infatuated. You start to imagine, for example, that someone to whom you are attracted finds you equally attractive. You indulge the thought in order to please yourself.

It's like scratching a mild itch. As you indulge in this fantasy, whether that person is attracted to you makes no difference, really, because it's your fantasy—independent of any basis in reality.

It feeds off scraps of conversation and pieces of experience; it becomes loyal. It's there every day, waiting to be fed and petted.

It's a feral emotion, something you don't let into the house to play with the other domestic emotions for the very reason that you know it's wild and that you haven't bothered to tame it or put it on a leash.

So it's dangerous. And fierce.

Then, in some dark part of your heart, you start to prefer it. You start feeding it from the table, giving it the best cuts, the tenderest bits. You act as if the story you've told yourself is true and thereby give it the power to disrupt the actual truth.

To be honest, I have trouble with the term "emotional affair." Is it the same thing as a passing fancy, a moment of foolishness, a silly crush? Then why dignify it with a term that sounds both romantic and pathological? At least the word "crush" sounds just about as ridiculous as it is, especially when applied to people who have credit lines, laugh lines, and party (or panty) lines.

In contrast to "crush," "emotional affair" sounds solemn and self-important. It doesn't want cheap hotels with day rates; it wants expensive lunches and love songs. It's got its head in a Nook instead of some nookie. Maybe the best thing to do with a crush is to laugh it back into perspective.

Remind yourself of Dorothy Parker's immortal line: "If nobody had ever learned to undress, very few people would be in love," which, of course, plays on La Rochefoucauld's "If nobody had ever learned to read, very few people would be in love." Recite these lines to yourself every four hours.

Crushes, after all, are like controlled substances: they can cure or kill depending on the situation, what they're mixed with—the technical word is "adulterated"—and in what amounts they're parceled out.

Use only as necessary; swiftly discard any unused portions.

18

Sixteen Things Women Hate to Hear (Even When We Like or Love You)

A convenient checklist of common phrases to avoid when in the company of women (including your wife, mother, sister, girlfriend):

1. "Relax."
2. "Can't you see that you're just torturing yourself for no reason?"
3. "Who taught you how to parallel park?"
4. "If you think it's worth it then I guess it must be worth it."
5. "Don't make such a big deal about everything."
6. "How could you *not* think that was absolutely hilarious? It was, hands-down, the funniest thing I've seen in my whole life. You have no sense of humor. Seriously."
7. "You already know how I feel about you. Why do you keep asking?"
8. "I'll get to it when I get to it."
9. "It's not a competition."
10. "Calm down."
11. "Next time, try buying shoes that fit."
12. "You look fine. It's not like you're the center of attention anyhow."

13. "I think a 'real feminist' wouldn't act the way you're acting."
14. "Get over it."
15. "Maybe that's what you heard, but it's not what I said."
16. "Whoa, you're so sensitive."

19

Sixteen Things Men Hate to Hear
(Even When They Like or Love Us)

Want to annoy the man in your life both instantly and profoundly? Want to make him wish he lived alone in the Fortress of Solitude or back in the one-room apartment he had when you first met? Say any of these well-known phrases on a regular basis:

1. "Tell me again: Why do you have to be friends with her if you don't have feelings for her anymore?"
2. "We need to talk. There's something I have to tell you and I've been thinking about how to say this for days."
3. "I might have thrown it away; I don't remember."
4. "That's not where my clitoris is and, umm, anyway, that's not how it's pronounced."
5. "Maybe I'd understand more about your work if you made the effort to explain it to me."
6. "Well, it made me and my friends laugh, so I thought you'd enjoy it, too. Why do you have to roll your eyes like I have no sense of humor?"
7. "A wittle baby-tawkie-walkie never hurt a big boy like you, you cutie nobbly-wobbly. Who cares if we're in a bar?"
8. "Just admit it: your mother and sister don't like me."

9. "Don't you know what today is?"
10. "How can they make you uncomfortable? It's not like they're hitting on *you*."
11. "I'm not saying we ever will move in together or get married, but if we do, I know I'd like this tablecloth."
12. "Of *course* I think your band/writing/animation/poetry/photography/idea for an app is good."
13. "How many people have you been with, anyway?"
14. "Come look at this hilarious thing about Ryan Gosling."
15. "Why does it bother you how I spend my money? You spend all your money on stuff that I think is a waste of time."
16. "Which of my friends would you sleep with if I died?"

You thought it was just women who found certain phrases annoying? (Yeah, right.)

20

The Truths About Relationships Nobody Wants to Admit

1. When you enter your next relationship, you become the person you split up with. Were you the parsimonious one, always pinching pennies and putting quarters in meters? Were you low on tips and tight on taxi fares? In your next relationship, you'll be giving twenties to maître d's and springing for indoor parking at the airport. Were you the tidy one, always doing the dishes? Your next squeeze will keep the kitchen clean enough for neurosurgery and you'll be accused of leaving too many coffee cups unwashed. Did you have to beg for affection, only to be told your significant other needed space? Just watch: you'll be the one craning your neck for a gulp of fresh air when the hugs are too frequent and fervid in this next situation.

2. One partner secretly believes the other is in control and wields most of the power. "I can't go anywhere without her knowing where I am and what I'm doing," he sighs; "He gets antsy if I spend too much time away from home and gets weirdly passive aggressive," she moans. Together, as if in a Broadway duet, they sing, "We always see your friends! Your family is the one who we have to work so hard to please that we never have any fun with them! You

make it so hard when we do what I want to do that we always end up doing what you want to do, even when it seems like we're doing what I want!"

3. It is not the "exact same" to be friends with people you had regular (or, even more strikingly, irregular) sex with as it is to be friends with people you never frame in an erotic manner. For example, erstwhile lovers tend to complicate conversations (or Facebook messages) with tiny smoke signals arising from their burnt bridges. The "what-ifs" and "if-onlys" and "who-knowses?" can appear like contrails, apparently out of the blue but actually evidence of a longer journey, above the heads and outside the horizon of the ordinary onlooker. Wistful is attractive in books, but in life, not so much.

4. If you have conversations about how you are, in fact, only "just friends," you are not "just friends." Friends don't have these conversations. I've had friends since junior high; we've talked a couple of times a week for forty years. Never have any of us felt a need to pronounce ourselves "just friends." It's not a topic for anybody except people who have the hots for each other. Don't kid yourself. Think about it: When dealing with your dentist, do you feel a need to announce, "You understand that we have a good working relationship but that it doesn't go any further?" Probably not. The phrase is shocking enough that one naturally avoids saying it to an individual holding a live drill in one's mouth. If that is indeed the case, and I maintain it is, why isn't it shocking enough to avoid saying to anybody with whom you're not eager to become intimately involved—or who isn't about to tell you to rinse and spit?

5. The French have a saying: "In every relationship, there is one who kisses and one who offers the cheek." One always loves more;

in every pair, one is reaching to offer and one is deciding whether or not to accept. Of course, the French also have tiny waists and that terrific custardy kind of quiche you simply can't find in America even at really good bakeries, so I'm not saying everything applies entirely to our culture. But I bet you'll agree that when gauging the romantic relationships of others, from short-term dalliances to long-term marriages (always hoping these do not exist simultaneously), it's easy to see who's the kisser and who's the kissee. Only in one's own relationship do things become foggy and are phrases such as, "We're absolutely balanced" or "We trade off; sometimes it's me, sometimes it's him" employed in all earnestness.

6. Love is a lot of trouble. But it's worth it.

21

Why Are Men Masters of the Breakfast Domain?

Why will men, including ones who don't cook any other meal, cheerfully make breakfast? Is it because if they make toast without burning it, it becomes "amazingly good toast"? Is it because when they add a "magic ingredient" (taco sauce) to their eggs, they can then call them "my mean scrambled eggs" or refer to themselves in the third person as "the Omelet Master"?

You know that if a guy can explain—without looking at notes from an electronic device—what it means to coddle an egg, he firmly believes he should have his own show on the Food Network.

Yes, of course I'm making sweeping gender-specific generalizations, but somebody's got to do it.

Besides, I really believe this one is true. Breakfast is the Man Meal.

My husband is one of the tribe: he makes scrambled eggs so good I believe they were a factor in my decision to marry him.

What made me hesitate briefly in that decision, however, was my husband's attempt to push his breakfast luck by going all out one morning and heating corned-beef hash in a microwave. He plopped the gray mass straight from the can onto a plate and then hit "reheat."

He looked smugly pleased with himself until he took the plate out of the microwave. The mess on it looked, and smelled, like offal. Instead of running for the hills—we have low hills near us anyway, so it wouldn't have done much good—I saw it as a teachable moment. I cooked the food properly, pointing out that hash can only be enjoyed when the edges are fried just enough to be crunchy. That's how my husband makes it now, because his "famous hash" is everybody's favorite.

Many men have a technique that they regard as their signature. They consider this to be an exact science as well as a huge accomplishment, the kind of which is usually accompanied by the sounding of French horns. This is true even if his signature dish is a bowl of cereal. I once knew a man who boasted that he made a "killer" bowl of cereal. He used soy milk and put pieces of banana on top. I suspect the banana is what made it "killer."

The pattern of men cooking breakfast on the weekends and getting a great deal of praise for it no doubt grew out of the McCall's-sponsored traditional ideology that suggested mothers and wives were responsible for making every other meal. Husbands were expected to return home after a long day's work and wives were expected, in exchange, to be waiting at the door with a cold martini (not one they've been drinking for an hour, either), with a perfect meal in the oven, and with cheerful children— already in their pajamas, ready to fall asleep at the drop of Daddy's hat.

Only on the weekends would the paterfamilias be able to exercise a measure of culinary creativity. One night he grilled and one morning he made breakfast.

He probably also encouraged everyone to gather round and watch him make breakfast; for men, being in the kitchen is a kind of performance art, says my friend Kim-Marie, requiring an audience for the full effect.

Another pal, Daniela, says her husband "stands at the stove the entire time, watching the food cook with his arms crossed over his chest till it's time to flip something over or move it around while browning. That's it; the entire time, he's standing there with the timer going instead of multitasking while the food cooks by, let's say, setting the table or making coffee."

However it's done, breakfast is worth doing.

Like love, breakfast is something people skip because they consider it more trouble than it's worth. Some folks think breakfast, like love, will keep them in the house longer than they'd like and will turn them into somebody sleepy and fat instead of somebody alert and lean. But that's not how it works. Both are fundamental: breakfast and love will nourish you even when you're busy doing other things; when they're healthy, they'll make every day better.

And like love, breakfast is best when made at home.

Or at a really good diner.

22

"Happily Married" Is Not an Oxymoron

Sometimes you feel like you've been married since the earth's crust cooled, but on other days when you look across the pillow or across the table and see your spouse, you probably are still amazed that you *have* a spouse.

Even when two people have made a terrific marriage, it doesn't mean there aren't times when it is simply flabbergasting to discover that you are married to *this* particular person. One likes cities; one prefers mountains. Or one likes skiing alone in the wilderness; one likes drinks before the ballet. One is a vegetarian; one's favorite saying is, "I'll have foie gras with the filet mignon."

Does that scenario sound too much like the theme song to the TV program *Green Acres*? Remember when Eddie Arnold sang, "You are my wife!" and Eva Gabor sang, "Good-bye, city life!" For those of us in the older crowd, however, the lyrics remain stupid but poignant.

And—I know this will come as a shock—it isn't only in television that couples have trouble aligning their interests and appetites. Let's put it this way: I've been married for a long time and there are days when I still wonder, "Excuse me, but who *is* this man?"

Here's the truth: I remember the first moment I saw Michael.

He came into the faculty lunchroom wearing a crisp blue suit during the spring semester of my first year of teaching. He'd been living out of town because he was on a sabbatical and was dropping by just to say "hi" after a meeting with a publisher. The rest of the English Department mob—all men except for me—teased him mercilessly for being nattily dressed. "Michael, did you just make your First Communion?" I think it was a former Department Chair who said that. They were torturing him in a display of masculine affection, but I decided to compliment the dapper colleague I'd never met before. His face lit up. Only after that were Michael and I formally introduced.

Six months later, he returned to his full-time teaching appointment in the English Department as I was beginning my second year as an assistant professor. Though he was twelve years my senior and an Americanist, we nevertheless had a lot in common: we were first-generation college students, neither of whose parents had completed high school; he was from New Jersey and I was from Brooklyn; we were both ambitious and wisecracking—and we were both going through divorces.

We got a house together three years after we met, renting it before we could own it and signing every contract for every book we could manage in order to put the cash together to make the purchase. I published a third book and got tenure. We celebrated our wedding in the still almost-bare living room.

The world was different in October of 1991.

On the night before our wedding, it was raining so hard that friends were navigating small, flooding country roads as if they were crossing the Atlantic without a compass, and given that we married over the Columbus Day weekend, this seemed particularly appropriate. Over pizza in our kitchen, two dozen friends and family were arguing about Anita Hill and Clarence Thomas. One of the friends was British author Fay Weldon, who had just flown over from London to "give me away." She figured out how to land an op-ed piece for that Sunday's *New York Times*, too, and was happily taking in all the talk of the election of this new Supreme Court judge along with her slice of pepperoni.

That night's discussion was riotously funny, focused as it was on sexual harassment, gender equity, and the question of whether women and men would ever understand each other. The next days these friends were summoned to help us (about an hour before the ceremony) in order to hang curtains in the living room because the fabric had only just arrived in the arms of other guests. The sound of electric drills securing last-minute changes to lighting fixtures accompanied the test of our new music system—we needed to make sure the cassette tapes worked, after all (ah, 1991)—and the pals who were preparing the food were having trouble remembering the recipe for ice.

One thing everybody remembers is that when I was coming down the stairs to my wedding song—"I Could Write a Book"—the smoke alarm from the kitchen suddenly began howling. There was a little problem with the stove; the ice recipe they'd mastered, but now cooking was an issue. So what's a little smoke? I sat on the stairs until Sarah Vaughan could be heard once more, and resumed my grand entrance. Instead of making a big deal about it, one of my relatives bellowed, "Oh, so it's one of those Italian weddings where the bride enters to a siren!" and we just kept going.

Everyone spoke and laughed, danced and ate. One friend reminded me of how terrified I was of moving to the country, fearful that I would have to garden. I told her that I still don't often venture off the deck, but that I cultivate other crops: Michael and I have, with growing skill and respect for patience, learned to make hay while the sun shines.

Actually, "Make Hay While the Sun Shines" is printed in bright red Art-Deco typeface across a vintage "sexy" postcard that I had framed for him on our anniversary a few years ago. I bought the card not because of the artist's rendering of a buxom dark-haired farm girl bending over a rake in a rather provocative (for 1930, at least) angle. (Not that I thought Michael would protest.) The card was perfect because we remind each other, maybe every other day, that life is short, that tomorrow is promised to no one, and that no moment should be willingly given up to sorrow or frustration.

"Make hay while the sun shines," I'll say if we decide to go out for pizza instead of cooking and eating leftovers after work. "Make hay while the sun shines," he'll chide me if I'm spending too much time in front of the computer screen instead of sitting on the back porch. We push and pull each other into joy, as well as into productivity and usefulness.

It's a good dance for a married couple, this pushing and pulling, this making hay.

Yet sometimes I feel as if introductions to my husband are still in order because I cannot believe I've contracted a lifelong relationship with somebody who (1) genuinely likes the Three Stooges; (2) searches the papers for "classic car" shows so that we may attend; (3) wrote a book on Henry David Thoreau; and (4) doesn't remember what "bracciole" is when it is mentioned on *Everybody Loves Raymond*, as if he's not married to a Sicilian. (OK, OK, so I've never actually made this delicious dish for my husband, but goodness knows I've ordered it dozens of times in restaurants and explained what it is in great detail—albeit with my mouth full. He should know by now; after all, he has no trouble remembering what a cannoli is and I've never made one of those, either.)

My husband, in turn, cannot believe he is married to a broad who (1) hates pie; (2) is scared to fly; (3) writes books and gives talks focusing on why the Three Stooges are a gender-specific hardwired taste and therefore untranslatable; and (4) can be counted on to laugh during the toughest time in a crisis but to weep (weep long and desperately) during TV commercials for long-distance carriers, cotton (the "fabric of your life" ones used to slay me), or pet foods designed for aging creatures.

But then there are the other times in long-term relationships that make it all worthwhile: there are the ones when you finish each other's sentences and the ones when you finish each other's drinks.

There are moments when the best thing in the world is knowing that somebody else understands exactly why you're laughing or crying and will join you or soothe you, whichever you need. The shared sly smile at the big dinner party indicating that you're amazed or appalled is a treasure. The delicious knowledge that you'll be able to talk about whatever happened on the way home, saving it up for later, is like a pilfered piece of dessert to share when you're alone together.

I believe it's that sense of being "alone together" that makes up for whatever is infuriating in a relationship. The phrase itself— "alone together"—is paradoxical, hard to explain, a little awkward, a little silly, and hard to understand.

Very much like a strong marriage itself.

23

Save the Last Class for Me

My husband is teaching a class on the poetry of Emily Dickinson this morning. He's been teaching Dickinson for forty years; it's not like there was a lot of prep involved.

But today is different for two reasons: Not only is it the last class of the semester; it's also the last class my husband, Michael Meyer, is going to teach.

After today—or, to be more precise, after next week's exams and grading—he will have retired from his work as a university professor. It's not like Michael's going out of business entirely, since he edits all those versions of *The Bedford Introduction to Literature* that you see everywhere, but he's done with the classroom part of it.

Maybe I should say he's done with the "office" part of it.

Michael has always been one of those teachers admired, respected, and (dare I say?) beloved by those he's taught; the Meyer Diaspora of successful former students offers testimony to that. And, from what those students who are taking his class this semester tell me, he hasn't lost his ability to captivate and inspire. He gives them a run for their money and they repeat his best lines over coffee. They can't believe he's been doing this since before their parents were born.

What they also can't believe is that the two of us are married to each other.

Michael looks and often sounds like an English professor out of central casting. This morning, for example, he left for work wearing a tweed jacket, blue shirt, and striped tie, with his briefcase firmly in hand. His salt-and-pepper beard was neatly combed, his dark eyebrows lifted in his usual expression of amusement, and his glasses were—as they always are—spotless. This is no crumpled academic. This is the Man. He's distinguished, handsome, and authoritative.

Me, I go to school looking like either Anna Magnani or Ethel Merman. After twenty-three years of teaching in Connecticut, I still look like I'm there to deliver a pizza rather than teach a class. I still sound like I'm from New York and I wear heels so that my students hear me clicking down the hall as I approach.

Michael and I are almost as different as it's possible to be and yet be part of the same department—let alone part of the same twenty-year marriage—so it's no wonder our students are shocked to discover we're together.

I know they'll miss him, as will our colleagues. Everyone could count on him to make them perk up, pay attention, and rise to the intellectual occasion.

That's why I think it was the "office" aspect of the profession, with its increasingly fill-this-form-before-you-say-or-do-anything, that drew him to retirement rather than any other kind of dissatisfaction.

Also, as Michael says, "It's time."

The son of a longshoreman and a factory worker, Michael's held a job since he was fifteen. He's now sixty-five. It's time to write, to read, and to drive with the top down.

After all, as a friend of ours said, "After you turn fifty, you're cramming for finals." Dickinson suggests as much in "Apparently with no surprise" when she writes about the inexorable and indifferent passage of time, as "The Sun proceeds unmoved/to measure off another Day."

Of course I'm looking forward to the next several years being as best described by the title of another Dickinson poem—"Wild Nights—Wild Nights!"

To my distinguished colleague: Congratulations on years well spent and classes well taught. Well done.

24

Relationships, Roundabouts, and Banana Boats

Here's what I've learned in twenty-three years of marriage: love isn't blind, but it is hard of hearing.

I said, *It's hard of hearing.*

At the beginning of a relationship, you hang on to each other's every word the way you hang on to each other's arms: more to display affection than to satisfy a real need. You laugh at every story and gasp in delight at every exaggerated tale. Every conversation begins a new pathway. Your heart beats faster when you hear your name or an endearment murmured by your beloved. You spend hours wondering whether you should repeat how much you care or if that would be overdoing it. Your sweetheart probably heard it the first time, but it might be worth repeating.

Then familiarity sets in and, like the foundation to a house, you settle into each other for better and worse. (In every relationship, it's always for better and worse: don't kid yourself that it's a multiple-choice question.)

You've learned every pause for comic effect and quirky inflection of the well-worn funny story. You know when an exaggeration is close to a fib and when a fib is close to a lie. Your heart beats faster when you hear your name or an endearment because it often precedes a request or a rebuke. If there's no answer when you shout, you wonder whether you should shout again or if that would be overdoing it.

You realize how important it is to be heard and how even more important it is to listen. Listening can't be overdone.

So you each listen and you both learn your cues.

In a good relationship, the dialogue always changes slightly, even when you're more or less rehearsing other conversations. If you're lucky, you're rarely playing to an empty house.

And at the best of times, in the most fortunate of lives, in the most hard-won, fiercely protected, and carefully cultivated relationships, there can come a time when you go beyond listening with your ears and know it in your bones.

It's not only about finishing each other's sentences, although that's part of it. It's knowing that the ground on which the foundation is built is unyielding; it's understanding that there are pathways to each other that rest beneath both of you like power lines, buried under the earth, unseen and silent.

There's an old joke about an aging couple. He wants to prove that his poor wife is losing her hearing. He decides to collect hard data to take to their family doctor. While she's cooking, he starts the test. Approaching her from the doorway without being seen, he asks, "What are we having for dinner tonight, honey?" No response. He moves ten feet closer and speaks louder. "What are we having for dinner tonight, honey?" Still nothing. She doesn't even turn around. He feels bad, but she needs to admit she has a problem. Finally, now standing no more than two feet behind her, he makes his final attempt. *"What are we having for dinner tonight, honey?"* he yells. *"For the third time already,"* she yells back, *"we're having chicken!"*

My husband has tinnitus, which used to be known as having "ringing in your ears" but is now defined as the perception of sound when no external sound is present. If you live with me, according to Michael, there is no such thing as having "no external sound present," but we're managing.

Sure, there are some odd conversations: On a recent holiday, he stopped to ask for driving directions.

A local woman told him to take the "roundabout." Only Michael heard what she said as "banana boat." She was pointing in the direction of a yellow building and he assumed that's what she meant. "Is that the banana boat?" he asked. She kept pointing to the traffic circle, trying to override his comment. "Roundabout! Go toward the roundabout!" "Banana boat? Is that the banana boat?" Finally, she just smiled and walked away.

As he told me the story, when he returned to the car, we were laughing so hard we were wiping tears from our eyes.

After twenty-three years, it turns out that conversations can become epic journeys (with some roundabouts). And the best parts are worth repeating—with bells on.

PART 3

Amateur Traumatics

25

Never Talk Politics with Your Family

If it weren't for our relatives, we might never have to be in the company of people we don't like.

Of course we *love* them, but relatives are an odd hybrid of those we simultaneously adore and discredit. We take them either too seriously (remembering sarcastic remarks for three generations) or not seriously at all (forgetting they're no longer married, or in the clergy, or both).

Had we met them in a non-familial setting, we'd probably make faces at them. Since we see them only a few times a year, we make nice.

Fate gives us relatives for one reason: so that we have to learn how to deal with people we'd otherwise never know. Would you really choose to have in your life the wily cousin, recently paroled, who is the last remaining adult man to drive a red Pinto? Why would you otherwise know a woman, your maternal aunt, whose dual passions in life are composting and the writing of villanelles? On what other occasion might you sit next to a person who, without apology, spends fifty-three minutes describing his recent toe surgery if not for the times you see your brother-in-law? Only family members inflict this kind of emotional untidiness on one another.

One thing to remember when it comes to celebrating the holidays together: heaven makes you family, but a new generation of selective serotonin reuptake inhibitors can make you friends.

I'd like to offer five suggestions for ways to make time with your extended family easier to manage:

1. Keep your mouth full at all times. That's right. Stuff your cheeks like a chipmunk. The more food you shovel into your craw, the less possibility there is of saying something inflammatory. Most family flare-ups occur when the emotional kindling that's been lying around for twenty or thirty years is lit by a spontaneous incendiary remark. Because it's impossible to say anything if your mouth is entirely filled by spiral-cut ham, green beans and onions, or tofu tempura other than "mrmph, mrmph, phuh," it's far less likely that you will be the cause of the family fight that will be remembered for three generations. So what if you end up looking like January Jones in that episode of *Mad Men* where she sported a "fat suit" that made her look like an actual human being? You can eat melba toast when you get home and risk being cranky only to your immediate household.

2. Either don't drink at all or drink often and early. If you're on those SSRIs, stay away from the Manischewitz and the Shiraz. And if you're the designated driver, do the same. But if you're going to drink, do it in a pleasant, easygoing, non–*Jersey Shore* kind of way. Don't drink in response—drink because you'd like to have a sip of something nice to go with your food. Don't drink because you want to put your brother's eye out with a fork.

3. If you want to put your brother's eye out, stay away from the cutlery drawer—and your brother.

4. Don't comment, even in a subtle way, on what you know to be other people's vulnerabilities. Whether or not you believe people can see you raising your virtual eyebrows, they can. Don't ask the cousin who's on parole, "Isn't it nice to wear something other than orange?" Don't ask the mother of triplets if she's going back to work soon because you've heard "it's hard for women to re-enter corporate life if they're away for more than six months." Don't ask your gay nephew, "Which of the guys on *Modern Family* would you rather date?" and then frown when he says, "Both."

5. Remember that you will never change anybody's mind about the following topics: politics, contraception, foreign versus domestic automobiles, country music, global warming, cats versus dogs, boxing, evolution, high-protein diets, texting, unions, Julia Roberts, religion, Jay Leno versus Conan O'Brien versus David Letterman, Jeggings, public education, ghosts, and primogeniture.

The best parts of any holiday are the serendipitous moments of laughter and connection not caught on video but recorded, indestructibly, in our hearts.

If that's not working, there's usually cake; remember suggestion No. 1.

26

Why Work Matters

"What's your goal in life?" I asked a cheerful young man at an alumni event. "I want to retire by thirty-five," was his snappy answer.

He smiled, cocked his head as if auditioning to play George Clooney's kid brother, and waited for what he clearly expected to be my delight. The line was rehearsed and he was close to twenty-five; obviously it had played well before other audiences.

I wasn't impressed.

"Let me put it another way," I said. "From what kind of work would you like to retire?"

"Something creative. Something where my passions and my talents are showcased. I don't want some soulless, mind-numbing office job."

"Ever had an office job? Is that how you know they're all soulless?"

"I don't need to do a nine-to-five to know it. Do you need to work in a factory or dig ditches to know those are jobs you wouldn't want?"

He wasn't necessarily a fool, this young man, but he was either ignorant or innocent—or both. And I thought about how his family, his college, and his culture had all failed him.

How can you be a good boss if you've never had one? Work absolutely is essential, not only for self-knowledge but also in pursuit of better communities.

By encouraging him to believe in his own exceptionalism, the adults who brought him up did him a disservice: by permitting him to believe, as the old expression put it, that the world owed him a living, they might have made it much more difficult for him to earn one.

That's why, instead of searching for his vocation, he was standing on the world's platform waiting for the Fame Train to arrive. He thought all he had to do was hail it by waving his arm.

This was not the scion of an aristocratic household, either, brought up by nannies and fawned over by tutors; this was a child of the suburbs, not of the landed gentry.

Yet he made it obvious that he was meant for greater things than everyday work. He made it clear he thought of tedious work as something done by others: by the ungifted, the ordinary, and the common.

His mistake about work is what's common.

My father worked in a small family factory with his brothers and brothers-in-law and a sister. When the place couldn't compete with larger companies, they went out of business and, at sixty, my father started working retail.

When he was very ill at the end of his life, I asked my father if he had any unfulfilled wishes, things he secretly would've liked to have done.

"I wish I could've been a mechanic." He shrugged. "I would've liked to work with cars."

His last dreams weren't about voyages or extravagances. They were about what other kind of hard work he would've done and how he might have liked it a little more. He would have preferred working on automobile engines to working on sewing machines.

People once talked about the dignity of labor. Now the word "labor" is usually associated with birth and "dignity" is usually associated with aging and death.

Birth and death are serious occasions, true, but work is also a big deal, or it should be. You spend more time at work than you do being born or dropping dead.

How can you tell that being able to get a job and to go to work is important? For much of history, women and those marginalized by the culture were prohibited from doing it.

Women, people of color, the very poor, and those seen as being of the "wrong" religion were barred from being able to walk through the gates and apply for work.

These jobs remained not as much out of reach as they were out-of-bounds. Laws had to be passed so that hardworking people would be permitted the privilege of being able to get them.

There were a lot of things I wanted to say to the graduate (including, of course, "One word: plastics"), but all I said was that getting a job he didn't like would still be better than hanging around hoping to be discovered. Work is an essential part of life's conversation. If you sit at the grown-ups' table, it should be an experience you are able to discuss firsthand.

It's OK if those hands are a little rough.

27

To a Young Friend Who Is Not Happy at Her Job

To a young friend who is not happy at her job:

You ask me if I ever felt the way you do now: Did I ever dread going to work even when the work wasn't demanding?

Oh yes.

I used to sit in the ladies' room at Bloomingdale's and count the minutes I was off the sales floor. If I could extract, with pay, a whole fifteen minutes, I felt a colossal sense of accomplishment.

I hated my job.

It was fine for the first few weeks. I liked getting the discount. I liked some of the ladies who'd been in retail for longer than I'd been alive. I even liked working in the particular area to which I'd been assigned: The Paradox Boutique.

Maybe they called it Paradox because nobody could figure out why anybody bought the items they carried. I sold leather miniskirts to old women who wanted to look young; I sold thirteen-year-old girls skintight spandex tops to make them look old; I sold drag queens glittering silky clothing that fit them perfectly and in which they looked better than any woman. (My senior colleagues had tutored me in how to look quickly for Adam's apples and large knuckles.)

I sold clothes by designers I'd never heard of but who nevertheless ruled fashion empires. I sold clothes that I would have never worn, even if I could have afforded $5,000 for a tank top. And I never, ever told anybody that something looked bad even when I wanted to run shrieking from the room yelling, "The horror! The horror!"

I worked on commission.

As I remember, I got 1 percent of every sale I closed. The work wasn't hard, yet I felt like I was doing time in a state penitentiary. I don't think I've ever spent so much time looking at my watch. (Ever notice there are no clocks in stores? It's like casinos; they don't want you to know how much time you've spent dropping your quarters.) All I wanted to know was the amount of my paycheck at the end of the week.

That's because the only reason I went to work was for the paycheck.

All my relatives spent their lives in either manufacturing or retail. The work was not unfamiliar. My father could sell the hell out of any window treatment, the more flounces the better. He got a kick out of it. Everybody who walked into the store ended up telling him the epic version of their life. He genuinely tried to find a swatch that would match the fabric of their life; he wanted to match the textile to the text. When his Parkinson's forced him to quit work, he missed going in every day because, as he put it, "It was like going to a club."

For me, spending fifteen minutes in a stall in the Bloomingdale's bathroom did not feel like going to a club. I felt like they owed me something, even though I wasn't exactly sure who "they" were. It was the same sense of disgruntled yet sanctimonious entitlement that drives people to take Post-it notes from work, extra fancy paper towels from expensive hotel restrooms, and Sweet'N Low from diners. You feel like you deserve more than what you're getting. You feel exploited, you feel stupid for letting this happen to you in the first place, and that makes you hate everything. Getting something from "them" is a way to feel like you got part of yourself back.

But it doesn't work.

(A student, with whom I was discussing this chapter, added a new generation's response to the disgruntled saga: "I smoked pot in the back room and ate as much free food as possible." Obviously she was working at a restaurant. Had I been allowed to work near food, I not only would have weighed 830 pounds, but I also would have figured out how to smuggle any non-perishable items into my studio apartment, which would have then looked like a fallout shelter.)

I'm saying all of this for two reasons: (1) everybody deserves a chance to find work that doesn't make them dread getting up in the morning; (2) everybody probably needs to go through the experience of having an entirely unsuitable job so that when a wonderfully suitable job comes along, they know how to tell the difference.

A suitable job is one where, even on a bad day, you know you're doing better than most. I told my young friend that when the best part of your workday is spent in the can, it's time to seek new employment.

28

Why I Hate Nature and Love *Electricity*

Forget the energy-saving-light-bulb crap. I'm getting a generator that can power all of Rhode Island. After having been without electricity for almost four days, I am swearing to the heavens (think Scarlett O'Hara "with God as my witness . . .") that I will no longer be without power when a storm strikes the Northeast.

Bring it on: tell me I'm a selfish, greedy, spoiled, bratty, useless suburbanite and I will tell you, "*Yessir, that's this baby.*" I am *not* trying to pass as something else. When the Apocalypse comes, you'll find me pushing Marie Antoinette out of the way and saying, "Let *me* eat cake! Forget them; I want the cake! Two helpings! I have some friends with me! Is there coffee with the cake, Marie? I'm just asking."

Life in the woods without electricity is really disgusting. Rustic, you say? Charming, you say? *Little House on the Prairie*, you say? More like *Gilligan's Island*, where my husband and I both want to be the Professor and nobody wants to be Mary Ann. The last time the power went out involved spoiled food—which is an anathema to this Italian girl, because it is a *sin* to waste food—and cooking on the Ironman grill. Actually, the grill business was OK until the french fries caught fire and turned into a potato-au-feu.

You could have put a tiny potato witch there and we could have played The Spanish Inquisition (you also need to entertain yourself when there are no movies and no television—and imagination leads to some bizarre places, like the creation of tiny potato witch hunts).

It was annoying to have no computer, no reading lights (those little bookmark things are fine for Steele on the plane but not for a serious article), and no water to flush the toilets except what we carried to the bathroom in buckets, but none of that compared to not taking a shower.

That was getting to be intolerable. I'd been mopping myself off with sponges and cloths and bottled water, but I was worried about just how effective my perfume was going to be—and my husband and I were starting to give each other that intimate look which translates into "Is that your smell or mine?"

When the power finally came on, I took a soaking forty-minute shower. It was like I'd just returned from forty-eight days in the space shuttle.

What did we learn from all of this? That we need to refine skills that will make us independent of the need for all this false, constructed, inhumanely modern contrivance that we call ordinary life?

No. It taught us that it is good to have generous friends with couches that become beds in New York City (NYC got the subways running again, but Connecticut couldn't get us a couple of watts?), because that's where we were headed if the power had not returned today, and it taught us to purchase, as soon as one becomes available, as big a honkin' generator as our great country manufactures.

Oh, and I did learn one more lesson: I should stop making fun of Nature. I wrote an article about how the storm was not going to be a big deal and clearly it annoyed Nature. Not that I'm being paranoid, but isn't it just a teensy bit odd that there are approximately 117 trees down on my street alone, all of which happened to fall on major power lines, while almost none of my more Nature-appreciating neighbors had damage?

I won't pretend to like Nature—it's too late for that—but I'll just be quiet about Her. Who knew She read my work?

29

Six Things You Need to Know About Changing Your Life

Life is like a great tailor: there's almost nothing you can't alter, but there's a cost for every alteration.

1. To change, to become different, you must *need* to change; you must have sought change for a very long time. A whim, a stretch of bad luck, a passing desire, is not enough. You have to know precisely what you need to change. And you must also know what you're willing to give—or give up—for it.

2. Glimpses of consciousness come at exceptional moments and are rare—for much of life, we remember only bits of things, moments at best. When you were a small child, you had all kinds of experiences: you learned your first words, you took your first step, but you don't remember those moments. Yet you can take for granted that they happened. These moments, as dramatic but immeasurable, take place every day.

3. There's enough going on in any one hour, let alone any one day, to occupy your senses and your imagination and keep you from asking the bigger questions. For some that's enough; they stay where they are and that is a happy ending. Getting to the end of each hour and each day is a sufficient accomplishment for them. But for others it's like living in one room of a ten-room house with the curtains drawn: for some of us, such self-limitation is a small, slow death.

4. Some parts of our lives leave only a trace while some cut a swath through our essential selves; you must decide which this is and act as you need to act. Ask your later self: "What do you think I should do?" Listen carefully. Your later self will answer and will tell you the hard truth.

5. With good change comes triumph: When you suddenly taste cream and realize you've been drinking skim milk all your life. You've been living in the straw house and finally move into the brick one where the wolf can't get at you. Nothing is more terrifying than hope. It's an investment: you always run the risk of losing it entirely. But it's useless to hang on to it and pretend it isn't there. There are few things in life worse than finding out something you thought was true was a lie. Just because you've become tired of emotion, or outgrown it, doesn't mean it'll be simple to free yourself from it. It must be dismantled, not ignored.

6. So change. You know you have to make your life different from what it is; you know you must not stay where you are unless you are willing to risk misery to yourself and to others who love you; you know you have the courage to do it if only you can rid yourself of the weight of the judgment of others. Your integrity must outweigh their censure and your dignity and fierce love of life must triumph over their most well-intentioned needs to keep you fastened to an existence that is no longer your destiny.

30

You're Not Perfect, Either, Lady!

I want to tell you a story.

When I was young and living on New York's Lafayette Street in a shabby, delightful, rent-stabilized apartment, the building's superintendent announced that everybody's windows were going to be replaced.

This information would not have been unwelcome—the old windows were made of creaky, swollen wood—except for one detail: the news was delivered in December.

It was an arctic winter, one of those tough years when Manhattan's tall buildings turn the streets into wind tunnels. It was bad window-replacing weather and could only have been the work of landlords who had just figured out that they were losing money by losing warmth. Maybe somebody smart actually explained to them how heat worked.

The impossibly bizarre idea of taking out and replacing all the windows in a three-floor apartment house during a series of snowstorms could only have been prompted by bad management and poor planning, as well as an almost-farcical disregard for the tenants.

I was living alone after my divorce at the time, but it didn't bother me that a bunch of guys were coming over to work in the apartment. It would be fine—they'd do their job and it would all be over soon. I made a big pot of coffee to show them some gratitude for their hard work.

Work hard they did: Four burly men removed the windows in a matter of minutes. The temperature in the apartment instantly dropped thirty degrees and snow started settling on the sills as they readied the replacements. Huffing and grunting, they lifted the new windows into place.

The new windows didn't fit into the frames.

The new windows were the wrong size.

The old windows, broken into unusable pieces, lay in heaps in the poorly lit hallway outside my apartment door.

We all looked at one another. The wind howled.

"We'll put some plastic sheeting over the windows," the head guy explained. "And we'll come back tomorrow."

The snow is blowing into my apartment. I live in a second-story apartment on the Lower East Side and all my windows are gone, and this guy says he'll put in plastic sheeting to get me through the night?

Not only would the place become an arctic wasteland within the hour; also, by dawn sixteen homeless people would be living with me, having made their way through the gaps in the plastic sheeting and set up, with full squatters' rights, a new life on my foldout couch.

That's when I started to yell.

I suggested that plastic sheeting over four windows would offer inadequate protection. I did not say it in those words.

There was silence.

Well, it wasn't really silent because the wind was picking up and some loose pieces of broken wood were banging against the empty window frames, as if signaling to the world that a single thirty-one-year-old was ready to receive all guests.

These four large men stood in front of me as I raved.

"How could you not make sure you had the right windows before you knocked out the old ones?" I used those words but added additional ones.

More silence.

Finally, the head guy paused before he finally met my eyes and barked, "You're not perfect, either, lady!"

That, friends, remains in my experience one of the most astonishing statements ever made to a disgruntled customer. "You're not perfect, either, lady!" "Yeah, that's true," I agreed, "but I didn't just go to *your* house, break your windows, and then suggest you sleep under a couple of extra blankets until tomorrow."

I must have looked as fierce as I felt, because within two hours they sent trucks to Queens, got new workmen from the Bronx, and installed perfectly fitted windows.

The lessons here? (1) You don't need to be perfect in order to insist that somebody treats you like a person; (2) learning how to raise hell is a useful and often-underrated skill, especially for women living alone; (3) just because you try to offer someone a warm greeting, it doesn't mean they won't leave you out in the cold.

31

Pack Only the Liberty Bag: Advice I'd Give to My Younger Self

Right before delivering a lecture at my old college, I stood in front of the mirror at the campus hotel and decided that the best way to prepare for this occasion was by cutting my hair with manicure scissors.

There, in my ancient, cracked, plastic kit bag, were scissors, singing their evil siren song to which no woman in her right mind ever succumbs, however tempting it is to "even things out" a little bit.

In that moment, I hesitated—not because I was miraculously overwhelmed by wisdom but because I was suddenly skeeved by the decrepit nature of my toiletry bag. Why was I using that? Why hadn't I thrown it away years ago?

Oh, right: I was still hauling it around because the one I'd bought from Liberty of London a couple of months ago was "too nice" to use.

As I turned on all the bathroom lights and narrowed my eyes in preparation for the first irrevocable snip, I saw, like a weird special effect, my own face as a girl.

My current face was no longer my face. It was once again the face with leaner contours, with wider eyes and a less practiced, more tentative smile. It was the face I used when looking out the sides of my eyes into the darkened windows of buses and subways to glimpse myself as others might see me, so that I could have a better idea of who I was. In those days I would glance out from underneath my eyelashes, practically making a pass at myself. I would try to shut my eyes almost all the way and stare in a mirror in order to have a sense of what I might look like when I was asleep.

What I wanted to look like as I slept was Ophelia in the Pre-Raphaelite painting, strong yet pitiful (I was taking art history). Or like the girl from *Last Tango in Paris*, sexual and dangerous (I was taking film studies). Or like Snow White in her glass coffin (I was crazy).

From that hotel room, close as it was to the dormitory where I lived from the ages of eighteen to twenty-one, it seemed as if I were looking into a face from another universe.

I was looking at a girl from a place and time when I believed a man might spend time watching me, examining me, as I slept, as if he were studying me for an exam. I actually thought guys did that on a regular basis. I even used to wear mascara to bed; I used to try to sleep on my back to avoid breathing on whatever young man was occupying the next pillow, in case my breath wasn't fresh.

I realized only later that if a man judges you by either your disheveled appearance or your breath after you've spent the night with him, you should not be agitated. You should get into counseling, change your number, and use bleach on the sheets.

The girl looking back at me from the mirror was disheveled, all right, but more on the within than without: she thought she was a tough cookie and a pushover; she was proud of her body but ashamed of her face; she wore no bra but spackled on her pancake makeup. She thought she was clever, not smart; funny, but not cheerful; appealing, but not lovable. She was genuinely friendly and deeply suspicious; fiercely ambitious and afraid to compete;

proud of her background but always frightened that her past (imagine, at eighteen, to think of having "a past") placed her, teetering, on the edge of disgrace.

She was afraid to get pregnant (only to discover later in life that she couldn't), afraid that everyone she loved at home would either die or get married if she moved away (some did, most didn't, and her presence would have had no effect either way), and equally afraid to fail and to succeed (failure meant you could never do what you wanted and success meant that you had a responsibility to keep succeeding).

What she never would have imagined was an older version of herself standing in front of a bathroom mirror at the College Inn deciding to cut her hair thirty minutes before delivering a lecture. In the diamond-hard arrogance of first youth, it would have been impossible to convince her that, in middle age, things such as hair might still matter.

I realized, as the trick of the mirror wore off, that I would tell that girl what she might well say to me: with the whole world to see, with everything important and joyful outside the window and not inside the mirror, put scissors, makeup, and fear into the beat-up bag and toss it.

Delight in chances, brought to us every moment like bushels of slurpy-ripe peaches, delivered fresh—every new hour of every day.

Pack only the Liberty bag. Wish good luck to the dead and the lost and understand that there is no sin except wasting time. Go outside. And play.

32

Shrinkage

There are certain things that I do for maintenance: I get a manicure once a month and I see my therapist about every six weeks. I am happy to say that, at this point, my nails crack more often than I do.

It wasn't like the therapists I've seen over the years have all been terrific, but in their own ways they've all been useful. Almost thirty years ago I started seeking help from an MSW in New York City, but we were never a good match. It was like being in a bad relationship, except that the guy could actually bill my health insurance company for lousy dates. It was a fraught time: I was ending a mistake of a first marriage, figuring out how to negotiate life as a newly single woman, and I was learning how to accept the demands of being an untenured full-time faculty member.

I was desperate to get tenure and to get it early. Nobody except my older brother understood what I was doing as a college professor. My father still hoped I would go to law school. When I finished my Ph.D. and landed a great job where I was teaching three days a week, he suggested I could work as a waitress the other two days. "Dad, I'm an assistant professor at the University of Connecticut!" I told him. He reminded me that waitressing was "an all-cash business" and, if I could work weekends, I could really rake it in, which might make up for the fact that I was only teaching three days a week, which he saw as a part-time gig. Meanwhile, I was finishing two books and moving between two states: literally between New York, where I lived, and Connecticut, where I taught, as well as moving between far more states of mind.

I also was doing this without the benefit of a driver's license. The only person over thirty in Connecticut not to have a driver's license, I discovered that I could not get a check cashed. Store clerks would accept only a driver's license as ID. This had never happened in New York. But when I couldn't offer a driver's license in the Nutmeg State, people looked at me as if I were an actual nut. The only reason not to have a driver's license if you live anywhere outside of NYC is apparently having been just released from a federal prison.

So, in addition to learning everything else new in my life, I was also learning to drive.

I think it was the idea of getting behind a wheel that actually drove me to see the shrink. I found myself waking up from dreams terrified that I would kill myself or others on the road, crossing lines or going off the edge. I don't remember who recommended this initial therapist to me, but I do remember thinking right from the beginning that he wasn't my ideal. First of all, he was too close to my age and I felt too competitive with him. I found myself trying to impress him with the work I was doing and with my own tough-cookie persona—neither of which was exactly helpful in approaching self-examination, let alone self-awareness. Yet, despite the ineffective nature of our interactions, there were two moments that make me think that, in retrospect, this relationship was indeed significant.

One is that he was the first person I ever spoke to about how much it bothered me that my face had been pockmarked by acne

as a teenager. This young man and I—we were both thirty at the
time—would sit in two chairs facing each other about four feet
apart, and I remember telling him, even though it was very hard
for me to say out loud, that one of the hardest things for me every
day was to look into the mirror and see my scars.

He was nodding and taking notes but after a few minutes looked
up and said, "What kind of scars are you talking about?" I felt my
face get hot from a sense of shame. I said, "The scars on my face,
of course," and I kept going.

He interrupted and asked, "Are they hidden by your hair?"

I said, "I'm talking about my skin."

He said, "I don't know what you're talking about. I don't see
any scars."

"I'm talking about how as a kid, I had such bad skin that when
I look in the mirror, all I see is the ravaged landscape that adoles-
cence left on me."

I was about to cry—I'd never cried in his office before and I did
not intend to start—and I was furious. I thought he was taunting
me. And I remember exactly what he said next, which was: "Whatever scars you're talking about are not ones on the outside. They're
not something anybody else can see."

And I believed him.

I believed him, but I stopped seeing him about six months
later.

I found another shrink, in Connecticut, closer to home. This
was another man, but a much older one and an actual psychiatrist.
I felt far more at ease. This man eventually ended up being dismissed on some kind of charges for being unprofessional—I don't
really know the details—but for me, he was life changing.

To give credit where it's due, perhaps the first therapist had
readied me in some way for the real work I needed to do.

Yet it's not as if I went into this new therapeutic relationship ready to be retailored into a perfect pattern of brilliant mental health.

Every patient tends to bury the most important story inside some other story, just the way new writers often "bury the lede." "Burying the lede" is an old journalism term for when you only find out what the real core or point of the narrative is about half-way into the article, but I think it also applies to therapy. It's when you start to explain what really matters to you when your hand is on the door and you're about to leave the office.

After several months of talking with this overworked new doctor, who was attached to a local hospital where he was responsible for dealing with the locked floor of a psych ward and haggard from overuse, I decided just as my fifty minutes were up to ask him the question that'd been on my mind my entire life: "Doctor," I said, "am I crazy?"

He looked up from his notepad so fast that his glasses fell down his nose and he barked out a, "Hah!" Then he said, quite simply, "I know crazy. You're not crazy."

His answer was both so abrupt and so wildly unprofessional that, once again, I believed what I was hearing.

I was willing to take his word for it that I didn't fall into that category. After he was dismissed from his post, I took a break.

It wasn't until I was in my early forties that I decided that I once again needed to get a better perspective on my life and refitted for my destiny, the way you might get refitted for a bra or a new pair of shoes.

At that point, I supposed I'd realized I was never going to have a house full of kids the way I'd always imagined I would but that I was having a kind of professional success that I never could have imagined. I felt profoundly guilty for both.

There were many other factors that made life great, but not easy: my marriage was strong, but life between two passionate, complicated people was never going to be carefree. In my academic life I had always made it my announced goal to make full professor before menopause, and I'd been awarded the designation of full professor before I turned forty.

But menopause had been trumped by an early hysterectomy—and that took some emotional recovery. In addition, my father was getting old and becoming ill. I was trying to figure out what losing my second parent was going to do to my life, even as I was trying to figure out how my father, my brother, and I could take care of one another through my father's final years.

When I was in my mid-forties, then, it was the graces or fates that brought me to my next and current therapist: I think we knew each other in another life, although past life regression isn't part of our treatment plan. I have known her longer than I knew my actual mother, but her presence is not maternal. Like the first therapist, she is almost the same age as I, but instead of feeling competitive, we have a sense of camaraderie. She holds an academic position, so we can speak in the shorthand of our profession; she doesn't ask why I don't waitress on the days I'm not teaching. We've now been doing these sessions long enough to be able to begin with the important work, instead of dancing around it.

With her, for example, I've learned that when I feel most vulnerable I appear most defiant and adopt the wheedling voice of a threatening and manipulative child. (This has not exactly helped me win friends and influence people.) I've learned that when I'm scared I get mean. I've learned to confront the anger, the reasons behind it, and manage my reactions to it. I've become less automatically defensive, which has permitted me to be more generous and, as a result, have a lot more fun. I've learned to say "thank you" and "I'm sorry" with a sincere heart and to say "I need more" and "I'm hurt" without flinching.

I've discovered that my apparent emotional honesty has hidden a great deal of emotional duplicity and that one of the reasons I have lived with fear as a constant companion is because I refused to shine bright lights into the dark corners of my past, where fear scuttles and crouches in the shadows. Only by bringing it to light can I unseat it in my imagination.

My therapist has helped me learn to understand that if you don't unpack your own emotional baggage it's no longer baggage— it's deadweight.

I see taking care of my emotional and mental health in the same way that I see taking care of a garment: After it's been through wear and tear, it needs attention and inevitably you're going to have to give it attention.

You can take to banging it repeatedly against a stone, as your ancestors did, or you can hang it up on a rope and whack it with a stick. That'll remove some of the debris away and shake things up, sure.

But it isn't thorough, it won't last long, and it's tough on the fibers holding everything together.

Or you can put it on the gentle cycle. The gentle cycle, you'll notice, is a cycle. It takes longer, it's got to be repeated, and you have to have patience.

I'm here to tell you it's worth it.

33

After Loss

My dear friend: I know this is going to be a tough holiday for you after everything that's happened this year. I can't say anything that will make it easier. Words, powerful as they are, can't change what you've had to live through. But I think it's important to tell you how much you mean to me—even if I have to use words both threadbare and weak.

When you've lost someone, every holiday you go through serves up fresh visions of what "might have been" and that's a killer. It's like being in a rattling old car, driving past houses in an affluent neighborhood, where the windows are all lit up, framing glittering parties. Or at least quiet, cozy evenings shared by lovers or families. And you're just out there, metal cold, going nowhere, afraid of breaking down, dreading the idea of knocking on one of those doors and asking for help. You aren't expected and haven't been invited; what help dare you ask for?

Even when you have been asked, it can be just as tough. Maybe you want company in theory but find the actual presence of well-wishers unnerving.

You know I'm accustomed to relying on a funny story or a

clipped comment to make my point. It's scary to leave those safety nets behind and walk out here on this emotional tightrope—my sense of balance and gift for being centered isn't all it used to be. I'm worried about making everything worse. But when I think of you waking up and getting through each day, knowing how much courage the simple gesture of getting out of bed takes, I am emboldened to take at least a small leap into unfamiliar territory and leave the funny stuff in the corner—just for now.

I know lights and celebrations and songs are not on your list this year.

You'll witness them because you have to—they are unavoidable. Other people's happiness is even more difficult to avoid than other people's pain. Seeing the holidays swirl around you means being hurt all over again.

Here's where life gets tricky. Few of us know how to offer kindness or generosity to a friend who is in pain or in trouble. Should we say something or leave the subject alone? Should we keep offering invitations, even if they are not accepted, or does that seem pushy and overbearing? Should we insist on coming over, dropping by, checking in, or is that invasive and bullying? If I were you, I'd be thinking, "Are you kidding? You're looking for a script? Do I have to deal with this stuff, too, on top of everything else? Don't you think it's just a bit much to expect me to take care of you, tell you what to do, make decisions about how I should be treated?" It seems like a bad joke itself, this fear that other people, people you love and respect, now have in your presence.

It makes being lonely and at a loss even tougher. I remember.

I remember my outrage at the awful normalcy of other people's lives; I remember feeling walled up inside myself, feeling the shortness of breath even as I added to the height and depth of my separation from others. I remember spending the holidays by myself, not because there weren't invitations, but because I recoiled from emotional pity and spiritual handouts more than isolation and sorrow. At least these last two were old companions.

But I also remember that often unexpectedly people could—sometimes with the simplest, most commonplace phrase—lift me out of myself. There was the December in England when, at the last minute, terrified of how far despair might drive me, I took the train to the house of a girl I knew from college. Never having met me before, her mother nevertheless did not hesitate in her welcome. No one expected much from me, but I was grateful to be part of the noises and gestures of everyday life. I'd almost forgotten that I once knew how to celebrate myself.

Every single day life is a privilege, a luxury, and, finally, the most extraordinary gift in the world. Because of what you are going through right now, you (as I) will always know this. These next few weeks will be hard, but you are loved, even if we who love you seem awkward and silly.

Together we ask everything that is good in heaven to be kind to you next year.

34

Spring Cleaning for the Soul

1. I will stop purchasing objects from flea markets, antique fairs, and online dealers in a thinly disguised quest for my long-lost and occasionally misspent youth. I will remind myself that buying a small, nearly empty bottle containing six whiffs of Evening in Paris cologne will not conjure up my robust aunts or miraculously manifest their soft padded shoulders against which I might fall into a dreamless sleep as I used to on Sunday afternoons. I will remind myself that possessing the midnight blue and silver-capped bottle will merely force me to regret spending more money on an empty vessel than they, in their frugality and wisdom, would have spent for a full one. In my life, not only do such items evoke my own mortality, but they also need dusting. Plus the more ridiculous of them make me recall vividly the phrase my beloved aunts uttered on a daily basis: "Gina, for a smart girl, you're not very bright."

2. I will stop hiding things to keep them safe. The one person from whom these purportedly valuable items remain hidden is me: I can never remember where I put something after I put it away for safe-keeping. I once hid a favorite necklace so effectively that I ended up begging every friend and family member to tear apart my clos-

ets, bookcases, and drawers to find it. My student Krissy lit candles to get the attention of Saint Anthony. And with everybody's help, including Krissy's pal Tony, I found the necklace. Now I keep it someplace easy for me to locate—around my neck.

3. I will stop collecting old grievances as if they were old perfume bottles or weirdly distorted Hummel figures. I will get over being indignant and I will shrug off being huffy. Impatience takes too much time, unfunny bitterness ruins the flavor of life, and resentment gives me lines that make my mouth go down at the edges, which is not a good look. I need this bad mojo even less than I need another empty bottle of Evening in Paris.

4. I will swear less.

5. I will remember to send greeting cards by mail with stamps from the U.S. Postal Service to friends and loved ones so that I might celebrate their birthdays, anniversaries, and happy occasions in a timely fashion rather than relying exclusively on Facebook. This way I will be able to acknowledge the happiest days of their lives before it is too late and without involving Mark Zuckerberg.

6. While we're on the mailing business, I will also write thank-you notes by hand and I will encourage any children and young people in my midst to do the same. I will communicate my understanding that a card's embossed "Thank You!" on the front does not mitigate my need to expand upon that sentiment in detail within the body of the text.

7. I will put my money where my mouth is and write checks to charitable organizations whose work I know and respect. Women need to understand the power of the purse. If we have the privilege, we should act collectively when it comes to choosing to write a check to a shelter or a local arts organization, for example, rather than buying another pair of shoes (or—you got it—tchotchke). Yes, donating time makes a difference, but so does donating thirty dollars, if you can afford it.

8. I will count my blessings when I am in the doldrums, count to ten when I am quarrelsome, and count on my friends when I need a laugh.

9. I will encourage in myself and in others a ferocious hunger for learning and an unquenchable need to be generous; I will celebrate whenever possible, reassure whenever necessary, and prevail even if it means being called bossy.

10. If I ever do buy Evening in Paris again, the bottle will be full.

35

Deal with Your "Emotional Allergies"

I was watching an episode of *Hoarders* during which a woman named Jahn whined, wept, and coerced everybody around her for almost the entire show. She terrified me to the point where I had to turn off the sound. It is precisely the way I react when scary movies get too much for me. I watched as Jahn's two adult daughters tried to help her understand her predicament. They struggled to help their beloved mother negotiate her emotional, financial, and practical issues—and watched as Jahn went from defiant and angry to the part that really spooked me: petulant, girlish manipulation. When her daughters said, at the very end of the show, that Jahn needed inpatient therapy, I wanted to cheer. And I thought, "Whoa, Gina, you gotta get out more and get less involved in these shows," but then I thought, "It's the whining. You feel sorry for every other poor soul on *Hoarders*, but you're allergic to whining."

It's like being allergic to shrimp or wool. OK, so it's not toxic, at least not literally. But I do sort of feel my throat closing up when I'm close to whining; there's even a physical component to the whole business. And I get itchy when I hear people do the Whine, just the way I do when I've got wool next to my skin.

So what can we do about our "emotional allergies"? Can we do more than avoid them or weed them out of relationship landscapes altogether? I mean, even if you're allergic to roses you might not want to eradicate them from the world's gardens, would you? Grab a tissue and let's see what we can do. . . .

Know your own limits and make them clear to others. When students come into my office to explain why their work might not be ready or up to standard, for example, I stop them the moment they start to whine. Before they can launch into any kind of a sad rationale or student sob story, I tell them that I am far more likely to respect what they're about to say if they offer a personal narrative that is straightforward and clearly stated. If the student bursts into tears, then I get out those tissues (see above) and listen carefully—but that indicates a very different state from that of a student who comes in to wheedle and coerce.

Give yourself several beats when provoked before you speak or react because you're reacting in a way that other people would see as an "overreaction." In much the same way that people who are not allergic to strawberries can eat them with abandon but those with an allergy need to monitor themselves if they indulge at all, you need to stop and think before you respond. You might not be able to control how deeply you react internally, but you can control how you react outwardly.

Desensitization can work if you can do it without too much resentment—meaning you have to want to feel more comfortable around people who push your most sensitive and irritated buttons. Often those who can push our buttons most effectively are those who installed them (Hi, Mom, Dad, sibs!), but as we all know, people can have their inner lives rewired. Usually with the help of a licensed professional, we can learn to erect useful and appropriate boundaries between ourselves and those who irritate us.

Don't test yourself unless you're ready to handle the emotional version of a "patch test." You know what a patch test is, right? It's the kind of thing that chemical products, such as hair coloring, always suggest to do before applying the stuff all over: you're supposed to find a small, unexposed bit of yourself on which you can gauge your reaction.

If you're going to be in the presence of the kind of person, or group, who drives you up the wall, make sure the wall has a door through which you can make a speedy exit.

36

Put the Brakes on Being Busy

The small kid in the bunny suit was deeply engrossed in an incessantly beeping tablet game when her mother asked her to pass the box of Cheerios to the cashier.

I was standing behind their cart with the *National Enquirer,* which was absorbing all my attention, until I heard the little girl reply in the kind of modulated tone usually associated with primetime TV news anchors, "I can't help, Mom. Can't you see I'm very busy?"

The mother and I made spontaneous eye contact. She automatically did the shoulder shrug, communicating, "Kids these days, huh?," and I smiled and nodded, silently responding, "Just imagine!"

But I also made a resolution: I'm going to banish the expression "I'm very busy" from my vocabulary.

If a six-year-old in a bunny suit feels she can claim that her demanding schedule doesn't allow her to participate in the lowly duties associated with shopping, then everybody is "very busy."

I'm taking that kid-on-the-tablet moment as a sign that we've gone too far in terms of using "I'm very busy" as a "Get Out of Being Polite/Considerate/Attentive Free!" card.

In America, when somebody asks us, "How are you?" we now yell, as if in a chorus, "Busy! I'm so busy, you wouldn't believe it. I'm not available to talk to you, for example."

Nobody says, "Fine. You?" anymore, because of how everybody is bustling. They've already bustled down the street as you've said, "Hello."

During the early eighties, our culture decided that the opposite of the word "occupied" wasn't "relaxed" but "vacant"—as if time were space. Maybe that's because people started using day planners to map out every hour. Those day planners made us feel like we had to fill each corner with the activity equivalent of knick-knacks in order to appear to have a life with no empty spaces.

We were counseled to manage our time instead of enjoy it. We organized our days into discrete productive units, checking off lists of tasks accomplished and goals met as if we had to prove ourselves to a cosmic parking lot attendant who would validate our life's ticket.

Not only was time like space; time was also money: we became increasingly complicit in the idea that the most important people had the least time to spend on the routines of ordinary life.

We made ourselves feel significant by believing that the busier we became, the more significant we were; the longer our to-do lists were, the more in-demand we were.

When was the last time when you asked anybody what he or she was doing and the answer was "not much," or even "nothing"?

That would be unnerving, wouldn't it? Wouldn't you get suspicious? Who's up to nothing? You would immediately start to think that person was up to something.

The only people who say "nothing" when asked what they're up to are mastermind criminals, international spies, and serial killers. You'd be tempted to call the FBI to look for duct-taped bodies in the basement or enriched uranium in the garage.

Being at the mercy of one's schedule is no better than being at the mercy of one's appetites, and it's not all that different: Despite protests to the contrary, we eat and schedule what we want, what we believe we need, and what we hope will satisfy us. It's not out of our hands; it's under our control.

So from now on, if someone asks how I am, I'll say, "I'm looking forward to summer," or, "I'm just about to have a slice of anchovy pizza, so life couldn't be better," or something else specific and cheerful.

I will stop saying that I'm "buried with work," "up to my neck in deadlines," or "swamped." I will stop saying my days are "insane," "nuts," or "crazy busy"; I will, in fact, dismiss any adjectival phrase that reflects on my mental health or anyone else's.

I'll put a stop to what my friend Meg Pearson points out is the most common of humble brags and I'll keep in mind what another pal, Helen Lukash, reminded me was Socrates' caveat: "Beware the barrenness of a busy life."

Here's my new motto: never be too occupied to be able to help the lady asking for the Cheerios.

37

Snappy Answers to Stupid Questions

Welcome to December! Get out the tissue paper and the bows. While you're at it, get out the tissues and the waterproof mascara. It's the holiday season, sweetie. Just face the fact that somebody in your family will make you cry before the month is out.

I don't care whether you're Christian, Jewish, Muslim, Hindu, Shinto, or a practicing atheist; if you're female and you have relatives, you'll be making weepy, baby-seal eyes at somebody's casual question while "I Saw Mommy Kissing Santa Claus" plays endlessly in the background.

The remark doesn't even have to be one of those deliberately loaded ones, such as "Three months' pregnant, or just going heavy on the gravy?," to hurt. It's enough for a random cousin to ask, "Any interesting vacation plans?" for you to hear an undercurrent that whispers, "Or are you still stuck with the mound of debt, those three unplanned children, and a house near the sinkhole?"

To prepare in advance for assaults both real and imagined, I asked my friends Sam and Antoinette to compile a series of replies to help the most fragile egos survive the rest of the year with the fewest tears—while having the most fun possible.

"Why Don't You Text like Everybody Else?"

    a. *"This probably never happened to you, but my friends and I talk face-to-face."*

    b. *"Why don't you have manners?"*

    c. *"Because I'm not so insecure that I have to bury myself in a three-by-four-inch piece of plastic when interacting with others."*

"Why Don't You Let Your Thirteen-Year-Old Date?"

    a. *"More importantly, can you now permit yours to leave the house without a parole officer present?"*

    b. *"Because I don't want him to end up taking a blood test on Maury."*

    c. *"I never thought to ask. But how are things between your daughter and what's-his-face? It is what's-his-face, right? I'm getting the name right?"*

"Are You Still Working at That Same Old Job?"

    a. *"I tried to quit, but my mortgage didn't magically disappear as I had hoped."*

    b. *"I'm sorry—I can't understand you with that silver spoon in your mouth."*

    c. *"Only when I get hungry."*

"Still Looking for Mr. Right?"

    a. *"Found him. But when I discovered his first name was Always I broke it off."*

    b. *"No, but if I see him I'll give him your number."*

    c. *"I'm actually looking for several. I want to star in my own series. You know any guys interested in being brother-husbands?"*

"Did You Remember to Bring Your Bathing Suit So We Can All Hit the Hot Tub?"
    a. *"Hit the hot tub? Sure, but I think a hammer would be more effective."*
    b. *"You want me to enter a body of water in midwinter? I think I'd rather hit you."*
    c. *"We can be close only if you keep your clothes on. And I bet I'm not the first person ever to say that to you, am I?"*

"How's That Diet Working Out?"
    a. *"Hasn't anyone explained to you that 'diet' and 'working out' are not words nice people use in public?"*
    b. *"Are you actually asking me that astonishingly embarrassing and incredibly intimate question? That would be like my asking your IQ!"*
    c. *"What diet? I got lipo. But I could only afford to get my earlobes done. That's working fabulously, as you can tell."*

"Don't You Love Those E-mails I've Been Sending You?"
    a. *"Sure! With all the thinking I've been doing, I need something intellectually appalling, sexually coy yet depraved, and wildly time-consuming to give my brain a rest."*
    b. *"Yes, and have you been enjoying my threats?"*
    c. *"Love them. Could you do me a favor and stand in front of that bull's-eye?"*

If you're faced with inquiries falling outside these categories, you can always rely on the two standard responses: "Wherever did you get this uncanny knack for always saying the wrong thing?" or "I'm sorry, I can't take my eyes off what appears to be an entire head of lettuce between your teeth."

Finally, dear readers, as my gift to you, feel free to use my all-time favorite line: "I'll forgive you for asking me that question if you'll forgive me for not answering."

PART 4

He Didn't Lead Me

into Temptation:

We Took a Shortcut

38

Bad Boyfriends at Any Age

All good boyfriends are the same. All Bad Boyfriends are bad in their own way.

That's why we need to understand them, even in retrospect.

To understand the Bad Boyfriend is to give him, paradoxically, less power.

It's time to tell the truth about Bad Boyfriends. After all, somebody should benefit from all that experience. I can't have gone through all that crap when I was young for nothing. To put it another way, women (and some men) should share our collective emotional databases so that we can be more fully equipped to handle our attractions—and our responses to those attractions. The Bad Boyfriend, whether you meet him at pre-K or at the assisted living center, can be defined as follows: he is the one who is able to make otherwise sensible girls/women *will* their own destruction and sacrifice themselves with the reckless abandon of hyenas at a kill.

Face it: A lot of women crave the Bad Boy. A great many otherwise sane women would confess, if given full immunity from our rational tsk-tsking selves, "That poor, tortured soul? I could work with him. He's got potential. Maybe I could get him to start journaling. Or scrapbooking. After all, he's creative, and I'm deeply attracted to creative types. I—and I alone—could discover the real reason for his inner sadness."

The Bad Boyfriend usually assumes a prominent position in our lives precisely because he's captured our imagination. We feel like he's got squatter's rights in our hearts. It's like he's a tenant in an apartment we're trying to clear out to set up a new household and he's the one who won't leave.

Want to know one of the reasons it happens and where the deeply tragic part of being a woman comes in? The bad boy was so much more interesting than the nice-guy heroes that there was no competition.

The Bad Boy, however, was somebody who would keep you up late talking on the phone long after the good boys went to bed early. Bad boys are the after-hours men. Wolfish in their appetites, brutal, determined, and sadistic, these antiheroes rage for freedom.

And let's not fool ourselves: Since little-girlhood, we're trained to find the Big Bad Wolf seductive. From Charlotte Brontë to Barbara Cartland, thousands of novels and tales insist that women have to find the man who will colonize their emotions, enslave their passions, and rule over their lives. In the name of finding love, women must seek out a fascist. Sylvia Plath wrote "Daddy," the definitive poem on the subject ("Every woman adores a Fascist")— right before she took her own life.

Somehow we haven't been able to fold him, like a minor ingredient, into our lives. He's like too much nutmeg or too much pepper. In excess, he wrecks the whole dish. If only we could have left the very memory or idea of him, everything would have been perfect. If only we could have become bored by him, fed up with him, immune to him, then he could have been filed among the happily ordinary boyfriends of the distant past. The weeks (or even, heaven help you, days) spent with the Bad Boyfriend leave a more lasting impression than the five years of your first marriage. You follow his movements and track his information as if by magnetic influence. You spend time looking up his old girlfriends on Facebook and the Internet to see whether they've named any children after him. You remember everywhere you went with him, every meal you had, how most arguments ended, and you can map out every vacation you took by remembering how many hotel pillows you cried into.

He changes with age.

Up to age twenty-one, the Bad Boy is at his most basic: he's hardly more than a child. Despite the fact that he has already passed his reproductive peak, his emotional fontanel has not closed. He has no idea who he is and he really has no idea who you are. Write this one off; reassure yourself that in better books the central characters are older than those in romance novels.

In his thirties, you're going to deal with the non-committal man as the Bad Boyfriend. He sees himself as vitally independent and suavely mature, which sets him up for a kind of guaranteed unreliability. Remember that anybody can be in a relationship if she's willing to be on somebody else's schedule, abide by somebody else's rules, and put up with somebody else's mess. Is that what you want?

At forty, the Bad Boyfriend is already committed; you're going to end up making out in a car like teenagers, which will be very exciting, except that there may well be baby toys on the backseat, which you are going to try to avoid letting into even your peripheral vision. The man who tells you what a terrific husband he is as he's putting his hand down your blouse is not a man you should trust.

In his fifties, it's the powerful man as the Bad Boyfriend. He has a lot of experience, which can be defined as "recognizes his mistakes as he starts committing them again." Secretly he thinks a twenty-seven-year-old might still fall for his charm and not for his bank account, status, or influence, and hopes never to have to settle for a woman his own age (whom he regards as far older in "women years").

At age sixty, it's the mature man as the Bad Boyfriend. His emotional fontanel has closed off, true, but so has the rest of his mind. This is somebody who's now figured out exactly who he is, which might allow him to be interested in who you are—but don't sell your condo yet. He expects you to offer him a lifetime achievement award.

At seventy-five plus, it's Grandpa as Bad Boyfriend. He wants a nurse with a purse: a woman who has her own money (so he doesn't worry about siphoning off his retirement, Social Security, or will) who'll be able to look after him in his "old age." She should have a loud voice, long legs, and a good hand for poker.

Having an unresolved Bad Boyfriend issue is like carrying around credit card debt. He's one of those store credit cards you only got to get the discount, which can still show up and wreck your rating. You hate the fact that no man was a Bad Boyfriend all the time. Wondering what you could have changed—you, him, the circumstances, his job, your family, the fact that he was twenty-six years younger than you, that he had a wife and sixteen children who looked exactly like him, that he was gay, that he was indifferent—drains your life like a vampire.

Even the memory of him remains tantalizingly out of reach. He's the man whom you're always afraid to see on the street, the one you're afraid that you're going to run into when your hair looks lousy, your nails aren't done, and you have a temporary cap on a front tooth.

The good boyfriend was happy with whatever you gave him. The bad boyfriend always wanted everything he could get.

That's what you wanted from him, too: everything you could

get. With a good boyfriend it was always easy to get fed up. He would always be giving and giving, but there would still never be enough of what you really needed.

It's like cheating yourself at cards, playing hide-and-seek alone, or buying a dress two sizes too big so you can feel small inside of it. The good boyfriend would be understanding. The Bad Boyfriend would be knowing.

The good boyfriend provided a nest or a ladder. With a Bad Boyfriend, you were always walking on a rope bridge. The Bad Boyfriend was hanging on to your hand as you hung over the abyss, and you weren't sure if he was going to let go.

From my Bad Boyfriends, I learned that life is not easy and that relationships are not always emotionally safe. From my good boyfriends, I learned an even more daunting lesson: that the very promise of safety is an illusion. I learned that while some choices seem less dangerous than others, life is not ultimately a game of tag. You're so thoroughly mind-numbingly dulled by your good boyfriend that the first time a bad boy with a sly grin rolls up his sleeves and looks your way, you throw your virtue, your conscience, and your sense of self-worth out the window along with your panties.

That's the double meaning of getting caught: getting caught is great if you're falling, but it's terrible if you're running away.

39

Ten Reasons to Thank the One Who Walked Out

1. He taught you that "boredom" is an anagram of "bedroom."

2. He helped you understand the importance of staying away from guys who play the opening chords to "Smoke on the Water" *all the time*, even when they are way past the bassist stage.

3. He helped you understand that for some men the phrase "sowing wild oats" actually means "always having a blonde bent over a coffee table."

4. You learned from him that there are insignificant others as well as significant others.

5. From him you learned that men fake sleep the way that women fake orgasms: to be left alone already.

6. You learned that a truly thoughtful lover would not attempt to arouse you with the subtlety of a chimp trying to dial a rotary phone.

7. He taught you that while breaking up might be hard to do, staying in a fundamentally miserable, spiritually chaotic, emotionally unsafe, and unutterably unfulfilling relationship was worse.

8. You learned, while being in that relationship, that someone else's suspicions can erode your own sense of trust and self-worth to the point where you doubt your sanity as well as your integrity.

9. Once you ended the relationship, you discovered that you no longer had to hide all your own stuff because he didn't like it, thereby happily freeing yourself from the "Repressed School of Interior Decoration."

10. All your previous boyfriends—good, bad, and indifferent—helped make you who you are today and who you are today is someone who can have an absolutely fabulous time tomorrow, if only you give yourself a chance.

The best thing to do with the Bad Boyfriend is to say "thanks," say "so long," and then wave good-bye.

40

When It's Over

How does it feel when a long relationship ends?

Imagine that he's the first one you ever fell for; he might not have been the first one to kiss you, but his was the first kiss to matter. You can still taste it. You remember the shock, and the softness, and the lingering of his mouth on yours. It was the first time you ever thought: "I want to keep this. This is mine."

He loves you. You can hardly believe it. He sends you little notes where he writes your name over and over again. He calls you first thing in the morning and last thing at night. Words, rolling dark as waves at midnight, wash over you; his voice is heavy and slow as he tells you that you alone understand, that you are the only one.

You can't believe it. You try to resist, not having been born yesterday, but it takes all of an instant for you to be swept off your feet. Swept off your feet, you lose all control over where you're going. Not that it matters. The undertow pulls the ground away and you drown. Willingly, entirely, without a last gasp or a hand raised to save yourself, you drown.

You are in over your head. You know it and still it doesn't matter. Not as long as you can stay immersed in him. You grow accustomed to this life, where shapes are never quite sharp and light is always refracted. Other voices that once called to you grow faint. The gestures you make are careful and labored, designed to keep you steady. They keep you where you are. Which is near him. Which is all that matters.

The day he stops loving you or, to be more specific, the day you realize he no longer loves you, you can't breathe. *What about when you no longer love him?*

The hurt is unfathomable. No one survives this. It would not be possible. You dive further down. The weight almost crushes you. It doesn't matter. Somewhere people are waking up, going to work, having lunch and dinner, sleeping through the night. You think of such a life the way a child thinks about castles and dragons; you can imagine it, but you know, somehow, that it isn't real. Such a life does not exist except in imagination. Maybe it did once. But not anymore.

Ignorant of your belief that time cannot pass, time passes.

Changes that you once fought against, tides that you swore did not exist, begin to move you. Very nearly against your will, if you claim any will at all, you are lifted and borne forward. The anchor you cursed as too weak to keep everything in place begins to seem like a gift, so easily does it break once you kick it away from you. It never was what kept you motionless. That was only your own wish to stay still, the way prey freezes in the gaze of the predator. That kind of stillness isn't quiet or safe; it is negation. Playing dead.

Moving again, you can no longer pass for dead. Re-entry isn't easy. The abyss was dreadful and easy. Being on your own two feet is not easy. Movement demands balance and choice. You thought you could get away with not having either. Thought that if you crouched down low enough, the current of change would pass over you. The sand on the ocean floor is not so low that it remains unmoved by change. How could you escape?

You go forward. You must. Even if you don't know where you are headed.

41

Timeline of a Breakup Recovery

You've seen those timelines illustrating how your health improves from the very moment you stop smoking, right? Such charts come from august groups like the American Cancer Society and prove that simply stopping something that's bad for you makes your life infinitely better.

Now, let's consider the idea of how leaving a bad boyfriend could improve one's life immediately—if one could just stop letting one's heart break over him.

(This would apply to anyone leaving a broken relationship, but I'll stick with heteronormative language here, since that's what I can best speak to from experience.)

Here, then, is my timeline, with associated benefits, for exiting a rotten relationship:

Within eight hours: Mascara stops running because fewer tears stream down face. Need for tissues decreases.

Within twelve hours: Desire to commit mayhem and throw objects decreases. Ability to form sentences not containing swearwords improves dramatically. Need to make sarcastic, critical, ironic, malicious, vengeful comments about everything in immediate environment becomes less constant.

Within twenty-four hours: Sniffling becomes intermittent, but savage ripping up of photographs increases.

Within twenty-four to thirty-six hours: Chance of making pitiful phone calls during the day decreases. Anger sets in, but ability to look in the mirror without weeping returns. Ability to shower and put on clean clothes increases. Need to talk about the horror of the relationship is almost impossible to stop. (Warn your friends.)

Within forty-eight hours: Ability to taste and smell improves. Anger is paired with increasing sense of relief and gradual reawakening of self-esteem. Chance of making bitter phone calls in the middle of the night decreases.

Within seven days: Full, restful sleep is again possible. Anger becomes tinged with ability to laugh at various relationship miseries. Friends no longer fear hysterical outbursts. Ability to move about in public increases.

Within one to three months: Circulation improves. Walking, eating, sleeping, and exercising all become easier. Chance of calling him up and slamming down phone without speaking significantly decreases.

Within three to nine months: Energy increases. Flirting becomes possible.

Within one year: Excess risk of heartbreak drops to near normal levels. New interests replace sense of being shackled to the past. Ability to see erstwhile lover in a crowd without gasping and weeping now possible.

Within two years: Wondering why it was ever such a big deal in the first place is typical here. Big miserable memories turn into little events you barely remember. You might even be able to recall certain moments with a smile, but let's not get ahead of ourselves here.

The important thing is this: you're healthy again.

42

Hearts and Parachutes

One of the worst breakups in literature occurs in *To the North,* an understated novel by British author Elizabeth Bowen. Emmeline, the central female character, faces the loss of the man she has come to desire, depend upon, and trust.

When she understands that he, after the long process of winning her over, is suddenly beginning the process of splitting with her, she recognizes at once that "[t]he dead stop of his tenderness, flicked off sharply as electricity, his incomprehension and ice-cold anger had given that hot bright Sunday . . . the lucidity of a nightmare." She realizes that her lover's "profound and slighting contempt for her point of view . . . must have underlain at all times his tenderness [and] was apparent in all that he said and did, most of all in silence."

To those of us who have experienced heartbreak, Emmeline's moment of recognition is terrible and terrifying.

I first read Elizabeth Bowen's novels in 1978, when I was twenty-one. I underlined the passages about Emmeline's disastrous love affair because I, too, was a young woman in love and I was desperately afraid I would never be as happy again. I wrote passages in my journals about how novelists hold grudges against true love and never let the vulnerable women win. I felt as if I were guarding my rights to happiness and pleasure, defending myself against my unseen enemies: a world of older people who thought they knew better.

I was lost to London; my heart was all in a fog.

I broke up with the boys I was dating back home because I fell in love, fully and entirely for the first time, with an English medical student who, with a felt-tip marker on my erasable noteboard wrote: "Now is the winter of our discontent / Made glorious summer by this daughter of New York."

We walked through Regent's Park. We went to pubs where I learned to drink shandies because they were cheap. We slept in a narrow single-student-sized bed where we fit together like spoons. I wrote long letters to my father describing the boy. My father replied in short notes—he hated to write—and said he hoped I knew what I was doing.

My older brother came to visit me in London for a week. Before going through the gate on his return flight, he kissed me on the cheek and said, "Don't come home."

I was happier in London than I had ever been and my brother could see it. My father could sense it. I suspected I would need to guard the feeling like a starving dog guards his food.

I was afraid of losing everything.

It was theft, and spoilage, and breakage, and disintegration I feared. I feared the howling sense of loss I associated with all change, even though change had brought me precisely the happiness I was frightened to lose.

It was late spring the first time I left London. Although I returned to England the next year, going to Cambridge, seeing more theater, and more of the medical student, I was right in thinking it would never be the same. I was never as happy in England again as I had been at twenty-one when I was scribbling lines from Bowen.

And yet, for years now, I have been far more happy, more consistently happy, and more thoroughly happy now that the first wear and tear (not waste, never waste) of youth is gone than I could have dreamed all those years ago. I know, it's not hip to be contented: I should be clawing at the gates of my own mortality or whatever one does when midlife is no longer mid.

But I did all that clawing and weeping when I was younger. I don't need to do it anymore.

You see, I was terrified of death and getting old before I turned forty. I was terrified of losing love the moment I felt it. It wasn't the boy—although he was lovely—but the awakening of myself that scared me. That sense of self is what I was afraid to lose, and I had attached it wholly (and mistakenly) to one young man because that was the only story of awakening I'd ever heard of. I didn't realize that falling in love was part of learning how to live my own life fully and not simply attach myself, like ivy or a barnacle, to a host object.

The young man and I grew apart despite the fact that I'd moved to England to attempt to make the relationship last forever. Winning a prestigious fellowship to Cambridge University and getting a graduate degree there was—I am slightly horrified to admit—more than anything else a way for me to be within calling distance of the boy for whom I cared so much.

Or that's what I believed at the time. But in fact my better sense of self, my better angels perhaps, permitted me to be more ambitious than I was willing to admit and to succeed at Cambridge even (and especially) when the relationship failed. If I had changed my life only to be with him, accepting a job I hated or that compromised me in some way, I don't know that I would have been able to get over the trauma of the loss as swiftly and entirely as I did. My relationship was crumbling, but my life went on. I'd struggled to find my own place, but it was my own place that offered me rescue when I needed it.

I am happier than that young girl in love ever imagined possible. I have found greater and more sustaining relationships because I have a better and stronger sense of my own self than I did back then—which, while unsurprising now, would have been impossible for her to imagine.

And so what I tell the younger—and not so much younger— people in my life who fear they'll never survive the loss of a true love is this: You can and, with help and time, you will. You'll be more generous, understanding, empathetic and less judgmental for having come through this experience. You'll be more flexible and less frantic. You'll be less innocent and more humble, which means you'll also be wiser.

And, with luck, you'll be more patient while being less of a pushover.

I would like to tell the girl with the leaking fountain pen and the cheap notebook from the local bookstore that she'll be all right. She was too afraid of losing what she had to be able to enjoy it fully.

I would tell her that hearts, like parachutes, are able to open fully more than once.

43

How to Get What You Want

Can you get what you want, no matter how personal, eccentric, or whimsical? If you want to wear a new pair of crystal earrings on your birthday, or eat handmade chocolates on Valentine's Day, or have a dozen red roses suffuse their seductive scent throughout your softly lit bedroom every month, can you be certain that this will happen?

Can these dreams and wishes be fulfilled?

And can you get all this without having an adoring and wealthy elderly suitor, or a trick pelvis, or both?

Absolutely!

Want to know the secret?

You get what you want for yourself.

You want flowers? Go to the florist. Go to the grocer. Go to your neighbor's hothouse in the middle of the night with a pair of shears and a flashlight—no, actually, don't do that. It will probably end badly.

But to expect the poor soul with whom you have an intimate relationship to read your mind will also end badly.

More often than not, you're thinking *"Swan Lake"* and he's thinking *"Duck Dynasty;"* you're thinking tea for two and he's thinking tee time; you're thinking about being swept off your feet and he's thinking about sweeping the whole ridiculous commercially fabricated romance ritual under the rug.

Let's use Valentine's Day as an example: from childhood on, many girls grow up with an almost-imbecilic fondness for February 14 that leaves most boys scratching their heads (at best) and making unseemly noises with a hand in their armpit (at worst).

I was of the girls smitten early. I remain smote.

I still send Valentine's Day cards to people: friends from high school and college, women I work with, some former students who are now pals, my nieces and nephew (all grown-ups), in-laws, neighbors, former colleagues, other family members (assorted), and, yes, my spouse. I like cards with glitter and I don't really care if the recipient hates glitter, which shows just what the Valentine's Day Madness can do to an otherwise empathetic and responsible woman.

If I want to send the card with the glittery princess on a sparkly pony holding a velvety heart, then, dammit, you'll open it and you'll like it. Or you'll throw it out. It actually doesn't matter, because the point was the pleasure I had in sending it.

"Pleasure" here, of course, is a term that demands explanation. I might have been weeping as I addressed the cards because of the Madness. I might well have been remembering the awful times I've had on this day in the past.

(I don't know many men who have this conversation, but I sure do know a lot of women who rehearse their bad Valentine experiences the way they talk about labor during childbirth.)

My worst Valentine's Day? Easy. I was living in London and adored a young man at the time. He had, for example, a British accent. It took me a while to realize that, in England, this was not exactly what you'd call unusual, but during that first infatuation I hadn't yet noticed. Anyway, he decided that the best way to spend the most officially romantic evening of the year would be to take me to a movie called *Zulu Dawn*.

I'm not kidding.

I still remember *Zulu Dawn*. I still have nightmares about *Zulu Dawn*. Let's just say that in handling matters of race it lacked the subtlety of, say, *12 Years a Slave* or, for that matter, *Django Unchained*. Maybe there have been more colonialist, patrician, and women-free films released by major studios, but I haven't seen them.

I most certainly haven't seen them on Valentine's Day.

What dawned on me back then was that I needed to take control of my life, wishes, and plans.

So that's what I do for Valentine's Day—and most other days, including weekdays and minor holidays. If I want to be happy, I rely on myself. If I want something, I get it for myself. This means I can be in the company of the person I love for the sheer delight of his company, which doesn't undermine romance but instead confirms independence.

And without independence, what's the fun of intimacy, after all?

PART 5

If You Run with a Bad Crowd, Can You Call it Exercise?

44

Why Friends Can (Sometimes) Be Better than Family

Everything I need to know in life I learned from my best friend. No, I didn't meet her in kindergarten, but we've known each other a very long time; I can't imagine what my life would have been like without her.

Even on a slow day, I'm pretty energetic—but whenever I see my friend I suddenly feel as if I've been half-asleep since the last time I was in her presence.

When we're in each other's company we're paying attention to details: everything is funnier and more interesting as well as worthy of discussion and comment.

We can count on each other for all the important stuff, whether we're facing the easiest times or the toughest times.

For example, I can call her at 10:00 p.m. in tears and know she'll stay up as long as it takes to get me calmed down. She won't mutter, "Do you know what time it is?" or "Do you realize I have to get up for an important meeting in the morning?" or "Can we talk about this another time? My show is just about to come on."

Having your good friend's phone number memorized or on speed dial is the emotional version of having 911 pre-programmed: you know immediately where to turn when real trouble happens.

Thank heaven I haven't had to make one of those calls in a while (knock on wood), but I certainly have in the past. During those long nights, it's crucial to know someone who cares about you will listen.

Not only will they listen: they'll listen without judging you. They'll listen and offer comfort without ever saying, "I told you so" or "I knew this would happen." In other words, they never sound like scolding parents.

In many ways, best friends say what you wish your parents might have said to you. After all, friends are part of the family you create instead of the family you're born into—and they can understand many aspects of your life that your own family members cannot or will not accept.

Women expect our best friends to be there in times of misery. We want to be able to contact our friends twenty-four hours a day, as if they were the fire department or QVC. I expect a great deal from my truly good friends—don't you? Don't you expect your friends to see straight through you—to look beyond the window dressing, or even the blackout curtains, to see what's really inside? Don't you expect your best friends to know not only how you like the furniture in the "public rooms" of your life arranged but also what you keep in the "junk drawers" of your life?

My friend, even though she would deny it, is smarter, funnier, braver, and more beautiful than she knows. It's also obvious, as soon as you meet us, that she is much kinder, more generous, and more giving than I could ever be (even on a major holiday). There's nobody in the world with her particular talents and strengths. Yet, like many extraordinary people, she shrugs off her magic as if it's nothing special.

As a friend, however, I take her gifts very seriously and celebrate them. I can lend her self-confidence, self-esteem, and a sense of accomplishment as easily as I can lend her a safety pin. That's

what friends do, right? When she needs to hear about the importance of what she does and who she is, I'm grateful to act as a cheering chorus. When I feel as if I'm wasting time, wasting space, and
spinning my wheels, she reminds me why putting words on paper,
or getting up in front of a group to speak, matters.

A good friend lets you know that you're not playing to an empty
house. Even if she lives hundreds or thousands of miles away—
or even if she's no longer in your life—she's cheering so loudly
and with such affection that you can hear her voice in your heart.

Through our best friends, we are rescued, repaired, and reju-
venated. May we always be able to rely on them and may we never
take them for granted.

45

And If You Envy Your Friend?

We expect our pals to soothe, comfort, and heal; basically, good friends are NEOSPORIN for the soul.

So why is it that we don't always trust our best friends with good news? Why is it often harder to announce, "I got a fabulous raise!" than it is to confess, "I took a cut in pay!"

Why is it that women lead conversations, even (or perhaps especially) with those closest to us, by rattling off our current insecurities and vulnerabilities?

Just listen to a woman welcoming another woman into her house. The place could be immaculate; you could perform neurosurgery on the floor. That's how clean it is. But she will always apologize for what a wreck the place is, right?

The stainless steel will be so brilliantly polished you can see through time, but she's showing you a cup left from this morning's coffee in the sink. You can't actually see the sink because of the glare from the shining plutonium fixtures, so she'll drag you over to prove that she's messy.

She believes she owes you an apology. All she sees is a mess. And believe me, she's not faking it. Women apologize and we mean it. But half the time we're apologizing for old stuff: the good host might really be seeing the chaos of the house she grew up in or worrying about the upstairs closet, which she is not going to show you. Or she might just be thinking about the unsorted and unruly nature of her inner life and believe that that's manifested somehow in her perfectly organized house.

Men? They don't apologize. A guy has a goat living in his house, eating the trash, and he tells you not to get in the goat's face because the goat has a bad temper. That's how he welcomes you to his home. (I'm not saying that men can't be neat. My husband's garage—yes, the garage is his, although my car is allowed to have sleepovers as long as it's clean and doesn't leave a wet patch—is as well kept as MOMA. He has art on the walls and tools are placed in alphabetical order. This is no man cave; this is a shrine to testosterone.)

The trouble is that every woman believes she got to where she is by pretending to be somebody she is not. And so we're uneasy. This uneasiness with our own success leads us to be uneasy with the success of our friends—especially our female friends. The shadow of our own self-doubt falls over them.

Is there an opposite of schadenfreude? You know, not where you're laughing at the misfortune of others, but you're feeling just a sneaking, small bit awful about the happiness of someone you otherwise adore?

I'm not talking about something as basic as envy; this is more complicated.

It's the feeling you get when your best friend is losing weight (when you're not), falls madly in love (when you're not), or wins Powerball (when you've been playing every week for twenty-six years and she bought one lousy ticket simply to break a twenty— not that you're bitter).

It's at these moments you offer one of those smiles so unnatural it looks as if it were put there by an undertaker. It expresses "I love you, but . . . why you? Why not me?"

I suspect that unworthy thought has crept, unbidden, into the hearts of saints. Unlike the cup in the sink, it's something for which we can't apologize.

46

Sitting Down with Your Demons

What wakes you up in the middle of the night, not in fear, but in the threshing buzz of low-grade panic?

Dread of being alone? Of getting older? Of illness? Of death? Of being unable to help alleviate the sadness of those close to you?

What's your demon?

I have a friend, a woman I consider one of the blessings in my life, who is facing a whole bunch of those nightmares. Her nightmares are sitting there at the kitchen table with her.

Maybe you know her; maybe you *are* her. Many of us have been where she is, in the dark night of the soul, at some point—but when you are inside the tumble and hiss of the bad time it is almost impossible to imagine rescue or survival.

But we, more or less, survive. Either the worst happens or it doesn't. We brush up against the savage edge of loss and cut ourselves, counting ourselves lucky to have been only scarred, only mangled.

Because there are worse possibilities: those times when you can't back away and you can't move out of range; the edge saws away until it can no longer be borne.

Or change the image. The hurricane that obliterates everything in its path goes through a place we once thought safe as if to teach one lesson: Nowhere is safe. At least not forever. At least not all the time. Happy times and bad times move through our lives like the weather. There are accurate predictions to be made, but there is nothing to be done when a force of nature moves in. You can see the horizon darkening, but whether you run to it or flee from it, you cannot change what will happen. You are stuck in that moment of time with only yourself as your shelter.

So what is there to say when someone you love is deep inside that storm?

Or change the image again—what is there to say when a friend is playing a part in a great tragedy on a stage too removed, too terrible, and too awesome for you to offer help? You can't shout out lines because the script is not yours to invent; you can't offer to replace her in the part because it is not your role. What is there to say that does not trivialize pain by offering sentimentality or that does not show disrespect by offering mere palliatives?

What I want to say to my friend is this: "I honor you as you move through this time. Not as a martyr or saint full of gracious sorrow, but as a fighter, as a warrior, as someone engaged in a contest for her soul, as someone who refuses to surrender to despair or to plot a coward's escape."

And I would remind her of an old story: Late one night, three demons decide to ambush a woman who lives alone. The three demons are manifestations of her worst nightmares: Fear, Anxiety, and Despair. They make a racket, breaking things, ruining what she holds dear, and disfiguring what she cherishes. Gleefully, they spend hours immersed in their rampage. They're enormously confident because they figure, "She's all alone and she's past her first youth, so why should we stop?"

They go at it for hours, into the darkest part of midnight. The woman they are tormenting is almost inconsequential; the destruction of her world has little to do with her.

When she starts to build a fire at the hearth, they barely glance over. But the demons become more thoroughly distracted when they notice that the woman is busily setting out a kettle.

Wary now, they ratchet up their activities. When she calmly sets out three cups, nevertheless, they stop in their tracks. Her hands aren't even shaking. She looks calm, if weary.

"What are you doing?" they cry in unison, breathless from their tasks of destruction. "We are everything in the world that is against you. Why are you boiling water and setting out dishes?"

The woman stares at them and gives a tolerant shake of her head as she opens the cupboard. "I know all of you by now. You've been here before and you'll be here again. You might as well make yourselves at home."

Raising one eyebrow and fully meeting their gazes without rancor, in full possession of herself, she asks familiarly, "What kind of tea would you like?"

47

Gifts of Omission

What three gifts were you given at birth? I'm not asking about your accomplishments or achievements. I'm certainly not asking what you made of yourself, but I am asking you to decide from what you were made.

What are your E-ZPass lanes? What can you speed through faster than anybody else? What are your get-out-of-jail-free cards?

Most of us wouldn't be able to claim, the way old-time Disney princesses could, that our fairy godmothers awarded us grace, sweet natures, and good looks.

Off-screen our gifts are—shall we say—more varied.

Mine, for example, can't be found on any gift registry. That's one reason it took me a long time to recognize them as the advantages that they are and admit that they're precisely the traits that make me who I am.

It turns out that my gifts, like my sins, are ones of omission.

It's not what I was born with that matters: it's what I was born without. Since infancy, I've had no shame, no fear of speaking up, and not even a hint of perfectionism.

So think for a moment (but not too long: this is about instinct) and decide what your fairy godmothers, or the genetic code, or fate gave you. What did the benefactors, before you were born, choose as factory-issued attributes you'd be given to help you get through life?

I asked my Facebook tribe this question and well over one hundred of them answered within twelve hours. I was surprised at the clear constellations visible from the pattern of their replies.

Most of them happily laid claim to a sense of humor, a talent for telling a story, and a willingness to make the best of a bad situation. They're grateful for their smarts, their resilience, and their health. They understand the privilege of being born into an environment where they can have legal access to education, to health care, and to free expression—aware that not only their ancestors but also many of their contemporaries around the world are denied these essential human rights.

A friend in Brooklyn admitted that her curly hair is a gift but explained it's also her curse. (If you have curly hair, you understand; if you don't, send me a stamped, self-addressed envelope and I'll explain.) My friend is proud of her facility for learning languages, because this has allowed her to travel easily as well as to live abroad, and she's relieved that her love of the water allows her to hit the pool without defining her beloved daily swims as mere exercise.

I'd see her gifts differently: I've known her for more than thirty-five years and I'd say it was her self-discipline—hard-won and diligently maintained—that makes her swim and makes her feel at home anywhere on the planet. The curly hair might count as a basic ingredient or an E-ZPass. The rest she's earned herself.

But I discovered that the best part of asking this question was hearing her say that she was proud of something—anything. If I'd asked her what made her spectacular or what she's better at than other people, she would have mumbled and denied that she could do anything apart from wake up, brush her teeth, and maybe—every once in a while when she could no longer make excuses—remind herself that she could still do a few laps without taking a break.

I think it's time to appreciate what we've got and what we've done with what we've been given.

If you're one of those people who can fix any engine, understand every piece of technology, or prepare a memorable feast from three chicken wings, two pieces of Gouda, and a leek, shouldn't you feel unapologetically grateful for these birthrights?

Think about giving somebody a present. Isn't it wonderful to see them use it? Isn't it sad to think that what you've chosen for them might be thrown into the back of a drawer, neglected, under-valued, or untouched?

Recognizing your talents doesn't mean believing they're limit-less. Accepting your strengths doesn't lead to pride but instead to humility; you're less likely to resent what others have if you understand your own bounty.

Self-acceptance? That's a real gift—whenever you receive it.

48

When a Friend Faces Divorce

What can I tell her, the friend who is facing divorce? There's nothing smart, funny, or original to say. But I've been her best friend for more than twenty-five years and I'm not about to become silent now, especially because I've faced what she's going through.

It's my job to say something, right? I can practically hear her holding her breath as she waits for fate, like a surgeon's knife, to cut her open.

What do I know, having gone through the experience? That even if what happens cures her, it will also scar her. Sometimes the two go together. Going through a divorce is one of those times.

She knows this. Impossible to tell her to shut her eyes and hope for the best. There's no anesthesia for the heart. You cannot cauterize your memories, burn away the worst parts by applying blades, or heat, or even an open flame. The only way to go through the experience of divorce is with your eyes wide open.

It's no Hallmark moment, no Kodak snapshot, and she will remember every detail—whether she wants to or not. Such places in our life's travels are revisited without albums or mementos. You don't need a souvenir to bring back the piercing sense of isolation from those days when you faced your soul's blank desert, when you peered into your heart's dark abyss.

Oh yeah, I'll cheer her right up if I keep thinking this way.

Part of the problem is that the divorce I went through has very little in common with the one she faces now. We had no children, no valuable property, and a brief common past; they have children and a house and have known each other most of their adult lives. Her situation is infinitely more complex and harder than mine was—and yet even mine was not easy.

I don't believe that there is such a thing as an "easy divorce." Even when I hear about barely recognizably human Hollywood types getting married in Vegas and then splitting up three days later, I think, "This is probably very tough for them." I imagine their sense of inner turmoil. These are folks for whom I would not normally feel a sense of sympathy. But when it comes to divorce I'm almost unnaturally sympathetic.

I bet very few people, even the frivolous, most superficial, most outrageous ones, say "I do" while secretly thinking, "I won't." People who get married think they will stay married.

Put it this way: very few people go up to the altar believing they are the one being sacrificed.

You have to make it work. What will your family think if you tell them you made a mistake as big as a bad marriage? What will your friends say when you become single again? Will you ever find someone better? Really?

It's very easy to scare yourself when you get close to the end of a marriage.

So you keep it going. You figure you'll settle for what you have (even if it isn't what you want), or get by with what you've got (even if it isn't enough), or ignore what's missing (even if you feel as if you're dying for the lack of it), or contort yourself into a wholly unfamiliar version of yourself so someone will stick around.

Except you know, in the most secret corner of your worst nightmare, that you cannot compel someone who no longer loves you to love you again. Maybe it happens on sleazy TV programs, in bad books, and in worse movies. But it rarely happens in real life—and I say "rarely" just to avoid arguments with those poor souls waist-deep in denial who believe that they have indeed reclaimed the true love of someone who once felt nothing but boredom or indifference. No matter what any talk-show therapist tells you, no matter what a self-help book you've read promises, the recovery of a lost love is as rare as the recovery of buried treasure.

What can I say to my friend? That pain is not our friend. Even if unhappiness is familiar, it should not be embraced. That she can change the habits of her life even though it seems impossible. Yes, some doors close and cannot be opened again. It isn't fair and it isn't right: that much is true. But it isn't all that is true. When you can't go back—and this is the good news—you move forward. Each day becomes an accomplishment, an extraordinary moment, an act of courage.

49

Girlfriends: As Essential as Cupcakes
and Revenge

There are three things only your real friends can do: tell you when your clothes don't fit, tell you when you're acting ridiculous, and help you celebrate something that benefits only you.

Strangers can tell you if you have spinach in your teeth. Somebody you've never met before can help you grieve. It's easier to offer an incidental observation or sincere sympathy than it is, for example, to offer authentic, enthusiastic cheer.

A stranger can indicate that you've got something in the corner of your eye by employing the universally recognized action of desperately rubbing the corner of her own eye until you, chimpanzee-like, mimic her action only to discover that you now have a flake of mascara the size of a tea bag smeared across the top of your cheekbone and resemble an NFL running back.

But only a real pal can tell you that your new iridescent eye shadow makes you look not like Katy Perry but like Tim Curry in *The Rocky Horror Picture Show*, only less subtle.

It's not easy to be a friend.

Oh sure, you can hit the "accept" button on a social media site and pretend to be popular, but does that really mean you'd be able to identify the person you just "friended" in a lineup? If you could, would you offer to make that person's bail?

A real friend offers bail.

Would you recognize his or her voice over the telephone? Even more important, if you saw on your caller ID that it was this person phoning you, would you pick up or let it go directly to voice mail? Real friends pick up and don't pretend not to know who it is.

Real friends say, "Oh, thank God it's *you*," and then admit who it is they are glad not to hear from ("The only time she ever calls is when she needs bail").

I know people claiming to have 3,236 friends who haven't had an actual conversation with a living adult in eight years. You know the kind I mean: the ones having five-second phone calls while texting, while waving to somebody while gesturing to you to "hold on, just one sec." You, meanwhile, are attempting to back away as quickly as possible from this carnival of self-aggrandizement. Sometimes they'll step on the cuff of your pants to keep you in place.

I always say, Lorelei Lee got it wrong in *Gentlemen Prefer Blondes*. It's not that diamonds are a girl's best friend, but it's your best friends who are your diamonds. It's your best friends who are supremely resilient, made under pressure, and of astonishing value. They're everlasting; they can cut glass if they need to.

Hold your friends close. Talk to them, in person if possible, and cheer them on. Real friends are a better—and kinder—reflection of you than any mirror. Friends are life's reward for getting it right.

PART 6

If You Met My Family,

You'd Understand

50

Why I Tell Stories

"You make a story out of everything," they told me when I was a kid, and it wasn't a compliment.

It meant I had a big mouth. It meant I wasn't good at secrets. But making up a story was the only way I knew how to translate pain into toughness, to turn a lie into an accomplishment, and to make something sad have a certain ending.

If you could make it into a story, you could make it into something that could stop. If you could make it into a story, it was yours.

Right next to the computer in my home office where I write almost every day is a "storytelling" award given to me by the Girl Scouts council for "empowering women through laughter." Inside a large gold frame is a four-inch, larger-than-life replica of a Girl Scout's badge where the words "Once upon a story . . ." are embroidered on the first page of a large open book. On top of its open pages lie an uncapped green fountain pen, a flurry of blue stars, and a golden wand of the kind usually associated with fairy godmothers.

The badge is pretty much my favorite item in the world. For me, it's like a seal of approval; I feel as if by magic it transformed a lifetime of fibbing into a respectable legacy of non-fiction narrative.

You see, I was never a Girl Scout. Where I came from, the phrase "What do you want, a badge?," while familiar, was meant to put you in your place and not to inspire ambition.

Since they were ubiquitous, the Girl Scouts probably existed in my old Brooklyn neighborhood, but my family was wary of any organization that involved putting on a uniform, showing up for scheduled meetings, and—this is probably the kicker—leaning on parents to volunteer. All of this meant that until I was thirty years old and took a job teaching in rural Connecticut I didn't know that trees had names. I thought a fire was something you set, not something you made.

This was a distinction I learned only when I accepted my Girl Scout award. When I was explaining the various benefits I would have accrued as a Scout, such as learning how to enjoy camping, which I still think of as "sleeping in the dirt," which is something my relatives did only a few generations ago, and which, as I recall, they did not recommend, I mentioned among these that I would have learned how to set a fire. There was one of those palpable pauses in the room, then laughter. What had I said? I was then gently corrected by one of the board members who explained that the preferred phrase was " 'make a fire,' or 'start a fire,' but not 'set a fire.' " I had not been fully alert to the nuances of incendiary language.

At the ceremony, I found myself emphasizing how much the badge meant to me precisely because the odds were so much against my getting it. Where I came from, they didn't call it storytelling— they called it lying.

That's not the whole truth of course. They also called it "making a big deal out of nothing, " "having a mouth on her," and "not being able to shut her up."

Simply because something is true doesn't mean it's a story, of course, just as adding a flourish to an event that actually happened doesn't mean you're a liar.

There are various kinds of tales, with lies and lessons falling somewhere on the storytelling spectrum.

I remember the first time I learned that adults lied to get what they wanted, for example. When I was about four years old, a neighbor's aunt took a bunch of us little girls to the local swimming pool, an outdoor chlorine pool surrounded by cement located in a large park nearby. This was an adventure. It might have been one of the first times I was ever out with a group that did not include a member of my own family. It was a warm and beautiful day; I was excited and happy.

But what I remember best was this lady lining us up, feet on the hot cement next to the kiddie section, and warning us in a low and scary voice that if we peed in the water, everybody would know because the park rangers had put in a chemical that would turn the water bright purple all around us.

Not only would it be embarrassing; the park people might also give her ticket or a fine. She might have to go to court over the purple water. She asked if we all understood and we nodded our heads in unison. She was terrifying. Of course we understood.

But as I said, it was a beautiful day and after being in the pool forever and not wanting to get out I peed just a little. I couldn't help myself. I realized what I'd done and closed my eyes, afraid to look at my shame, and waited for everybody else to scream. Nothing happened. Nobody noticed anything because there was no purple stain. The aunt kept reading on the lounge chair, not looking up from her magazine. Everybody kept splashing and yelling. Everything stayed exactly the same.

For me, it was a triumph as well as an epiphany to discover that adults might hold things over your head, but that for all their convincing intimidation and authority, it doesn't mean they're telling the truth.

The threatened consequences don't always get played out.

You don't get pregnant the first time you have sex as a teenager.
Your partner doesn't always know if you're having an affair.
And you don't always get caught if you cheat on your taxes.
Or set a fire.
Although, of course, sometimes you do.
But that's a different story.

51

Marrying Italian

"Never marry an Italian," advised my mother, who herself had done exactly that. Never once did I point out that, as my father's child, I was part Italian myself and that in marrying me someone would have to ignore what my mother regarded as a universal maxim.

After all, wasn't I hoping someone else would not take her seriously? If everyone followed her advice, then who would marry me?

Not only didn't I marry Italian; I didn't even date Italian, so powerful was my mother's warning—and the warnings from other women in the family whose legacy of distrust was handed down to me like a recipe.

Don't get me wrong: the men in our family were not louts or creeps. They were handsome, charming, smart, and perceptive. In addition to being adoring of women generally, they were able to make any woman on earth feel as if she were the only object of significance in the universe.

They were not like the *'Mericanos* of their own age—American men whose most seductive line was "Aww, honey, c'mon." Among Italians were men who spun the words of love the way they might knead dough for pastry, sip the wine made in the basement, or flavor the gravy with fresh basil: patience and timing were crucial.

You had to love what you were doing and focus on almost nothing else while you were doing it. No wonder the local girls lined up to date my cousins; no wonder the married ladies in the neighborhood would hang around when my uncles (or my father, for that matter) spent hot summer days painting the house or working on the roof.

Certainly I was under their spell. They told me I looked like a doll, like a princess, like an angel. I soaked up every word, purring and preening. Only after I heard these words repeated, syllable for syllable, to an out-of-town second cousin did I start to question their veracity. This cousin, who had a nose so big you could use it to dig a foundation and eyes that popped out of her head, was *also* "a doll," "a princess," and "an angel." I was about ten years old and it was probably the first time I raised my hand (palm facing my face, until parallel to my forehead) in a characteristic Sicilian gesture and said under my breath, "Che fai?" ("What are you doing?"). How could my uncles say to her what they had always said to *me*, testimonies of love I considered were mine alone? How could they compare the two of us? How could they act as if I was special when, it was now clear, *everybody* was special—which meant that nobody was?

Only later did I decipher the secret code directing how such men lived and loved: you told people what they wanted to hear. There was no reason ever to do anything else. The little girl wants to hear she's beautiful? Of course she's a great beauty—what lady isn't? This braggart wants to hear that he's the head of a wonderful business, that he has become the most admirable of men? Go ahead; tell him he's a champ. Who's it gonna hurt? Praise his car and his house. Make his day. Your wife or your girlfriend (or both) wants to hear that you love her more than anything, that you would die without her, that she is the only one who understands who you really are? What are you going to say? When she's looking at you, imploring, needing only a few words to make her happy, when a phrase or two will wash all worry from her face, what are you going to say? Of course you love her, only her, forever her. When you say it, you mean it. Just as you mean it when you say, every Sunday, "This is absolutely the best meal I ever had in my life." Who can say the happiness of the moment doesn't make the words true?

Whatever she said, my mother would look at my father with laughter in her eyes. Wanting to protect me from the sadness in her life (she had learned that my father's declarations of love were not for her alone), she also warned me away from what had once made her happy because she feared I would be hurt if that joy was then diminished, tarnished, or lost, as hers had been.

But my husband (a blend of French, Irish, and Norwegian) swears that marrying Italian is the best thing he ever did.

Who am I to disagree?

52

"Listen to This One. . . ."

For a while now, I've been having this recurring dream where—
Have you stopped reading yet?

If you're a guy, I bet you have.

If you're a woman, I bet you're saying, "Oh, please, just wait until you hear my recurring dream! I've had it since I was six. It only happens if I'm stressed or I've eaten cilantro. Fresh cilantro. The dried stuff doesn't do anything and it's never really as good; I don't care what they say. But tell me about yours first because my dream takes a long time."

If there are any men still left in the room, by this point they're tying ropes to lighting fixtures because they're planning to hang themselves. They're thinking that death might well be quicker and probably significantly more pleasant than waiting for these two to stop talking about what happened while they were asleep.

Haven't you found men to be less than fascinated by the detailed recollections of the unconscious and haphazard experiences that constitute dreams? For a few years, I had a male shrink. Even he didn't want to hear my dreams.

And when recurring dreams happen over, say, ten, twenty, or even thirty years of marriage and are ritually recited over breakfast as if they were they were somehow "breaking news," I've known men to get downright irritated and take their coffee to another room.

(That's where he is now: the other room. I told my husband what I was writing about and he decided to go to an entirely different section of the house. It's not as if I were reading out loud or sounding out my words. I wasn't asking him how to spell "labyrinth" or "polyp"—although both appear regularly in the dream, in case you're interested.)

Men don't want to hear about dreams. When somebody says, "I was playing Barbies with Madeleine Albright and we were in either a circus or a brothel when suddenly I started to cut my hair with manicure scissors and Albright says, 'Shouldn't a priest read you your rights before he hears your confession?,' which is what she always says in the dream, but this time I answered, 'These are not my walls, but my paintings are on them,'" the natural question is, "What do you think it means?"

And a lot of men don't like to analyze things.

I've rarely encountered that problem with women: We crave the kind of weird details dreams deliver. We want to hear when old boyfriends and dead relatives show up; we want to decipher possible prognostications and omens.

Maybe this reflects my Sicilian and French-Canadian background—maybe WASPs haven't done this kind of thing since Hawthorne was writing—but my aunts used to gather over morning coffee and talk over their nocturnal visions the way Wall Street financiers talk about the market forecasts.

In part, they also did it for the same reason: They would play any combination of numbers that appeared in somebody's dream. Aunt Rose would start, "Last night, I was back at 3072 Emmons Avenue," and before she could get in another word Aunt Clara would yell, "I'm playing those numbers! They're mine!"

Since most of the family lived in walk-up tenements, I don't think dreams turned out to be as reliable an economic indicator as either, say, the Dow Jones or the price of copper futures (which the aunts measured by use of the penny jar), but that didn't undermine the seriousness or regularity of the daily review.

It also didn't prevent them from regarding any information they received from the "other side" as entirely reliable.

Somebody dreamed a toddler died in a car accident? That poor kid didn't leave the house for a month. The fact that he didn't die was then used as proof—proof you could not dispute—that the dream saved his life.

I used to think that was hilarious. Now, if I have a dream about falling down the stairs, I hold on to banisters.

Perhaps the dreams that come to us even while we're in this mortal coil should at least occasionally give us pause—if only just long enough to write down the numbers.

(Look who's come back into the room. Hi, honey!)

53

My Mother's Dreams

My mother's anxiety dreams were filled with images of herself ar-
riving at the airport, bags packed, ticket in hand, only to remember
that she had forgotten something: She didn't have her passport, or
her pills, or she'd left one of the kids alone in the car. She had to
go back.

Her head was in the air—she loved the few times she'd trav-
eled on planes, feeling independent and sophisticated—so it is not
surprising that her dreams would be filled with plans for travel.
And yet even in her dreams my mother made it to the airport but
missed the plane.

Maybe what she actually felt was that she had missed the boat.

Married at twenty-three to my father, who brought her down
from Quebec to live among his tribe on Ocean Avenue in Brooklyn, my mother felt both lucky and unlucky for the entirety of her
brief life. She and my father genuinely loved each other, I believe,
but that didn't guarantee happiness for either of them. They were
ill-suited, love or no love.

My father wanted what all men want: a woman who did not
become irritating, weepy, and untidy as soon as her emotions were
engaged. My mother wanted what all women want: to be cherished

by a man strong enough to sustain the force of her inner life once it was revealed to him in all its passion.

What happened to them happens sooner or later to most human beings: they learned that a lover, a spouse, is different from what they had imagined. Usually it takes a long time for this discovery to be made. Some people make it in a week. I think it took my parents about five years.

For the first five years they seemed, by all accounts, very happy; when my older brother, my father's namesake, was little there were outings recorded by home movies. One of the family's prized possessions was a little black disc, a "record" made at Coney Island in which my brother sings the theme song of the TV show *Davy Crockett* ("King of the wild frontier," croons my brother, as only a kid raised on the asphalt of the city can croon the words "wild frontier").

But when I appeared several years later the few extant photographs show me and my brother, or me and my grandma, or me and the flowering crabapple tree in the tiny backyard. Certainly there are no snapshots of the four of us together. My mother stopped wanting to have her picture taken because she thought she'd lost her looks.

That her once-glossy blonde hair had turned dull and brown was not helped by the fact that it was cut with her own scissors to save the expense of a beauty parlor. And she'd put on weight; of course she'd put on weight. She had two kids, lived in a huge family where the only thing that mattered was food, and she hated going outside. Clothes were no longer new or crisp.

She retreated. She was ashamed. She usually waved away the camera—that much I remember—and the few times she posed for a picture she looked nothing like herself. In a rare new Easter outfit or about to go to somebody's wedding, she was all dressed up, carrying white gloves and a black purse, unsmiling, head tilted in a way to disguise what she probably feared was the beginning of a double chin.

I barely recognize her.

By that time, she was perhaps no longer herself. Maybe that's why she was always dreaming of escape: planes on the tarmac with their propellers already turning.

My mother thought being married would change her life, and it did. But when a woman looks to a man to change her life, she looks in the wrong direction. Not that she, as a poor woman without an education, had much of a choice in 1951.

Prevented from mapping out a course for herself, she was swept up by the current of her husband's life, out to sea without a compass or chart. When she signaled for help, it looked like she was waving at the shore. It hurts me to think that, alone and panicked, she wondered why no one came to the rescue.

Few choices were offered to women such as my mother, so maybe she was fortunate. Two or three times, at least, she had managed to take off.

I think of her every time I fly.

In my dreams, I am coming home.

54

Sex Talk in the Park

My mother decided I needed to have the where-babies-come-from talk when I was about five years old.

I remember the scene vividly: Mom and I were in a local park on an asphalt-shimmering summer day. As usual, I was playing on the grass with a large, grubby doll named Tootles. Tootles pretty much looked like the spawn of Satan, since I'd hacked her hair off, chewed on her hands, and partially enucleated her, but she remained my most adored object.

And as usual, Mom sat on a bench with a paperback from the library open on her lap, smoking and watching people pass by. A skinny young man headed toward us, running his fingers through his hair. He was followed by a heavily pregnant woman who was shouting at him through her tears. He did not turn around to answer her, but neither did he abandon her altogether. He walked just far enough ahead to be out of reach.

"Poor girl," said my mother to no one in particular, which meant I was supposed to respond even if I didn't understand. "He's not good husband material." In those days, women spoke about men as if they were cut from bolts of cloth. "But at least she had a wedding ring on. That's good because she's going to have that baby in about fifteen minutes." My mother took another puff on her Lucky.

"I'm not going to get married," I announced in my most grownup voice, shoving a small rock into Tootles' ear. "I'm just gonna have babies and not have a husband."

That's when my mother decided we needed to have the sex talk.

We were in a loud, busy public park; it was about a hundred degrees outside; I had no idea what I'd said to upset her, but it was clear from her expression that upset was what she was.

She grabbed me from the ground and sat me next to her, looking into my eyes. "You can't have a baby without a husband. Don't ever say that. Don't let anybody hear you say that."

I didn't like her tone. I put the doll between us and said, "I'll just go to church and pray for one. I can have a baby without a husband if I pray enough." I waited. Nothing.

Then I decided to use my clincher. "I'll make a novena."

I had no idea what that meant, either, but I knew it was powerful.

I picked up words the way seagulls picked up shiny objects: not because I understood their significance but because I liked their texture and their glitter.

"Gina," answered my mother, who never used my name in ordinary conversation, "you can't have a baby without a husband because to have a baby you have to have sex with a man. And you can't have sex with a man unless you're married to him. Do you even know what sex is?"

It was my turn to say nothing.

Then she explained. She used words I later realized she mispronounced in her heavy Quebecois accent, probably because she never said them out loud (at least, not to anyone who would correct her). English was not her first language. Explaining to her kindergarten-age daughter the physical details about sexual relations probably wasn't exactly part of her first language, either.

I was stunned. I had no idea what on earth she was talking about. I'd never seen a man or a boy naked. It was as if she were talking about life on another planet or like something out of Dr. Seuss or *Alice in Wonderland:* weird and unnatural.

She talked for a long time. I stopped listening long before she was done. She was trying to be thorough and precise, but I gave up any attempt to follow because I was becoming more confused with every word.

Many women my age have similar stories; many men my age had their own, often equally unnerving and more misleading, introductions to the story of sex.

Younger people, those under forty-five, have far different experiences. Some are worse, but most are better: for the most part, they are taught the names of their body parts (and the body parts of others) from toddlerhood onward. Their stories about the where-babies-come-from are cuter and sweeter because they are less infused with shame and fear.

What we learn and how we learn it matters; my mother was hoping to protect me from the kind of ignorance that would lead to a life of crying after men who would walk away in a hurry and remain out of reach. I suspect she was also trying to help me avoid a life of sitting alone on a bench, smoking, and talking to nobody in particular.

55

When a Mother Doesn't Like Being a Mom

Dear Mom,

I don't know how you did it. Your life wasn't easy and I'm not sure you actually liked being a mother.

I'm not making a rebuke; after all these years, after all you went through and all I've been through, that you might not have enjoyed your time as a parent is an observation I'm offering as a way to understand you better.

Robert Louis Stevenson, the Victorian author of *Treasure Island* and *Dr. Jekyll and Mr. Hyde*, declared in a letter: "The children of lovers are orphans." I believe he's right.

Maybe that was part of it.

You and my father had loved each other once, fiercely and wildly for your day, with a courtship taking place between Quebec City and Brooklyn when there were only back roads for Dad to make the long drive in an old Buick to visit you.

When I was fifteen and a boy I liked who'd moved upstate wanted to see me again, you were emphatically against it. "No young man drives for hours just to say 'hello' and go for a walk," you insisted. Your green eyes narrowed and you searched for a mirrored understanding that I didn't yet have.

But from that conversation I learned two things: this guy's visit was out, and Dad probably hadn't made those trips for just a cup of coffee and a stroll through the Plains of Abraham, a park in Quebec City.

You gave up your family and your mother tongue to be his wife. He was dark and handsome, recently home from being on a B-24 in World War II. He brought you to live with his mother and sisters in the noisy, crowded three-family house where they spoke in a Sicilian dialect.

But because you loved each other and wanted to be together, you made compromises and made a family.

But then your life got hard. Your husband was not a good husband; you couldn't tolerate his infidelities the way Italian wives in the neighborhood had learned to ignore when their own husbands stepped out on Friday nights. You became overwhelmed by a sense of loss and somewhere in the confusion of those times— even in bad times not every day is bad—became pregnant with me.

It wasn't the right time for another child. You told me that the aunts were horrified when you announced you were expecting again. Dad spent more time away from home. You weren't able to eat some of your favorite foods (I didn't like cucumbers or ham even in utero, apparently) and you added pounds you were never able to lose.

Interfering with your marriage and your life in both tangible and profound ways, I don't think it was simple for you to love me.

And my father adored me, and I him, which didn't make it any easier. You were a great reader, your eighth-grade education notwithstanding, and within my hearing you once laughed about how right Freud was right about mothers and sons and fathers and daughters. I didn't understand what you were saying, but I remembered the line until I could find out what you meant, because I spent my childhood trying to decode you.

You loved my father, true, but because he had caused you such profound despair, it pained you to see him loved by anyone else. Even his children.

You couldn't leave him because mothers didn't do that, because there was nowhere to go, and because, after all, you were married to the husband you'd chosen.

I tried to make you happy. I learned to tell stories and be funny in order to cheer you. The smiles and laughter I wrought are moments I remember with joy; the skill has served me well to this day.

I did my best, Mom, and I know you did yours. What else could anyone ask from either of us?

56

Questions I Wish I'd Asked

Oh, my old friend . . .

You ask me to remember what it was like for me when I was sixteen and my mother was dying. Your friend has a daughter the same age and what worries her most is leaving her child: What should she be explaining to her, telling her, advising her?

You ask me what questions I wish I could have asked my own sad mother, who checked out of her life at forty-seven as if checking out of a rented room.

So here are my questions, straight from the heart, no fancy talk, no wish-I-were-more-tender-or-loving, no emotional editing. What's clichéd is clichéd; what might seem overwrought is merely hard-won. It's uncut, like a bad movie or (I hear) good dope.

Love you.

G

—

Questions for Mom

1. I'll think of you every day. We'll always have a relationship even when you're not here. So what little thing, what tiny, ordinary detail, would you like to serve as your bookmark? When I

see a black butterfly, when I hear a door slam, when I smell coffee? When I hear a certain piece of music, a scene from a movie, a TV character? I'll be looking for you everywhere. Please give me a hint about where you'd like me to find you.

2. How can I honor you? In all the big ways, of course, by being a good person, by being brave and loving and smart and having integrity and all that, but how about in smaller ways? Would you like me to dedicate a book to you, write a song for you, a play for you, start a scholarship in your name, volunteer at a school and dedicate that time in your name, paint a picture with your portrait at the center?

3. What stories would you most like me to tell about you? What stories can I tell about us? I'll talk about you all the time. Of these stories, which is the most important to you? All of them are great, but which make you laugh the most or mean the most to you? Is it when I was very little or when I started school or when my brother and I were playing or when you and Dad talked about me? How did you think of me when you first started to see that I was different from you? How are we most alike? What stories show those parts, our likenesses and our differences?

4. I'll always remember those days when I could have done more for you. Is there anything you might want to say to an older version of me who might feel bad that she wasn't mature enough to be even more focused? Can you reassure me that I've been a good daughter even if I'm not the best daughter in the whole world— because that's impossible?

5. Do you think if we were the same age—if you were my age now or if you'd known me when I was grown-up—that we'd be friends?

6. Is there anything I've ever said to you that you'd like me to say again? Because not only will I say it right now; I promise I'll say it all the time and that you can listen for it wherever you happen to be.

7. What do I need to apologize for? How did I hurt you and how can I best ask for forgiveness?

8. You don't mind that I'm not going with you right now, do you? You don't mind that you're going on your own? Is there a way to let me know that I don't have to feel bad about hanging out here?

57

What Makes an Apology Real?

What goes into the perfect apology? My family wasn't big on apologies. There was too much pride, too much hurt, and too little empathy. We made up for it by being big on guilt and denial.

Living on the Lower East Side of emotional life, in the push-cart section where everybody held on to a bundle of emotional baggage, we never unpacked our grievances and we never put them down.

Of course, if you never unpack it, it isn't really baggage, is it? It's just a heavy weight you carry around.

There were aunts who held the pink slip to their spouses' souls, never quite forgiving them but instead showing them their ever-open wound whenever some heft was necessary to win an argument.

These were men who wanted nothing more than a chance to prove themselves reformed or remorseful, but the aunts wouldn't permit it. Instead they seethed and settled down into smug procrastination; they patented the art of being patient, wounded, and "excused" from life the way sick kids are excused from gym.

Is it a surprise that such unconscious stratagems don't exactly increase intimacy? A conversation that includes the lines "What else do you want from me? How many times can I say I'm sorry?" rarely ends with a cuddle and a smooch.

I was raised that way and it's a tough habit to break.

People seek forgiveness for lots of reasons: They are tired of the oppressive nature of their wrongdoing; they would make life easier for themselves; they want to make life better for others.

They want to go to heaven. Even if they're not sure there's a heaven, they don't want to go to hell. They want to get rid of a shadow life, they want to express their sorrow for pain they caused, and they want to air out every piece of dirty laundry.

Or maybe self-reproach overwhelms them. Guilt is like prickly heat; it's rarely fatal, but it sure is uncomfortable. Some people can stand it while others are driven almost crazy by it.

Is there ever a time when one person's need for forgiveness or confession overrides the other person's need not to be hurt?

"No," says my friend Maggie Mitchell. Author of the literary thriller *Pretty Is*, where questions of guilt and innocence abound, Mitchell argues: "If your apology is driven by a desire for forgiveness, you're not only missing the point but probably compounding the original offense: It's still all about you."

But two other friends disagree. Melissa Baartman Mork explains, "The offender doesn't need to receive the forgiveness. The offended needs to forgive." And Kathleen Thompson reminded me, "Forgiveness isn't earned. It is given by choice."

That's probably a reason it was hard for my family to seek forgiveness: we were big on earning but not on receiving.

If forgiveness was a gift, then it had one strike against it.

We were encouraged to be wary of anything simply given to us. What looks like a generous offering might be an act of war. Hey, the Trojans learned that the hard way: they should have looked that gift horse in the mouth.

But lately I've discovered that saying "I'm sorry" is not mere window dressing but instead is the only way to keep some doors from slamming in your face.

Here's what an apology isn't: an apology is not an excuse; it's not an explanation; it's not a justification; it doesn't come attached to a return-receipt request.

The person asking for forgiveness should not be tempted to provide a context whereupon the recipient of the apology is supposed to then feel sorry for the offender. An apology does not blame the victim (which is what the bankrupt and meaningless line "I'm sorry you feel that way" does) but instead comes from a willingness to humble oneself and to accept responsibility.

And you can't ask for forgiveness with your hand either in a fist or around a noose; you can't threaten or cajole others or yourself in the process.

Yet a heartfelt apology and sincere forgiveness can both offer a way to conclude life's unfinished business: there's a reason the word "end" is tucked into "amend."

58

"You Think I Have All Day?"

I no longer have any idea whether or not I was a good daughter to my father. After my mother died, he took on the tough job of raising a teenage daughter who was still in high school. It wasn't what he'd signed up for, but he made good on the contract and we did well by each other.

And it seems to me that good daughters would have insisted on their beloved aging parent moving in with them or, at the very least, would spend most of their days making soup and changing sheets when he was dying of what he had named his Trifecta: Parkinson's, epilepsy, and cancer.

Instead, I called every night no matter where I was and checked in. I visited once a week or once every ten days; it took me three hours each way, which was too far to be easy but not far enough to be difficult.

My brother was with my father far more often, in part because he lived only twenty minutes away but mostly because he had risen to the occasion. It was my brother who accepted responsibility for the day-to-day running of my father's existence as he died.

My brother did the real work, wheeling my father from 17th Street up to the cancer center on 34th because my father was too crumpled, his body too unyielding, his fear of physical pain too great, for him to be loaded into a taxi. It was my brother who took him for chemo and radiation, making the seventeen-block wheelchair trek in the snow, in the rain, before the sun was up, as if my father were a letter that my brother, the undaunted postal carrier, was entrusted to deliver.

The part my father hated most about being in the Army Air Forces was not that people were shooting at him, but that somebody else had the right to tell him when to wake up, or go to sleep, or have a smoke. At the end of his life, there were healthcare aides taking care of him and so, by necessity, telling him when to eat, sleep, and take his medication. Seneca, the philosopher, once said: "Sometimes in seeking to escape our fate, we leap to meet it." My father, who never remarried after my mother died in 1974 because he didn't want to end up being beholden to anybody, ended up being dependent on everybody.

The last time I went to the city to see my dad, it was 101 degrees. I had a small suitcase containing frozen lasagna, which I brought to tempt my father's diminishing appetite. My brother, my father, and I met at NYU so we could all talk to the oncologist.

When I'm in Manhattan, I usually have a sense that whatever I'm doing, somebody else within thirty blocks is doing the same thing.

Not that day. For once I was sui generis. Even in Manhattan, there weren't too many middle-aged women wheeling frozen lasagna around town as a sort of votive offering to the gods of illness and old age.

Maybe you know what it's like dealing with a loved one who's very sick; many, many people in the world do. We just don't do a very good job of talking about it.

Loving a very sick person, loving someone who is dying, is like taking somebody to the train station where you're supposed to drop them off, say your fondest farewells, and wave good-bye from the platform as they head out on the next part of their journey.

You think you know what's going to happen.

But you don't.

Because it's like getting to the station and seeing that their train has been delayed. You don't know when they'll be leaving and you sit around waiting for the departure, not knowing quite what to say apart from the usual comments about whether the bags are packed, what they enjoyed about their visit, and what they think about where they're going. For the last year of his life, I sat next to my father, looking up at the departures board so that we could both figure out when he was actually going to get on that train.

And my father was the consummate New Yorker: never in his life was he patient. He died at the age of eighty-four having never learned that particular virtue.

To be honest, our family never considered patience a virtue. Patience, we thought, was for people who didn't have enough to do. Patience indicated, we thought, a lack of imagination. Patience was, in our unspoken but shared assumption, the minimum wage of virtues: it hung out, did as little as possible, and still got rewarded.

For my father, the Third Avenue bus was always too slow. The line at Met Foods never moved fast enough. Even the microwave took so long to heat soup he'd swear at it and mutter, "At least with a pot, you get to stir. You don't just stand around like a moron." He spent his life rolling his eyes and saying out of the side of his mouth, "C'mon already. I don't have all day."

The photographs of him from his time in the service—he flew twenty-three combat missions—show him sitting around with a bunch of other boys smoking and laughing. He looks happy and anxious. Though he was stationed in England and in Italy, the backdrop never seems to change. There are some Liberator bombers on the tarmac behind him; the sun is always shining; his curly black hair is slicked back and short; his teeth look very white in his bright smile.

But in his eyes I see a familiar look: He'd rather be in that plane than on the ground. He'd rather get it over with than wait for it. He'd rather be terrified and active than serene and passive. He wasn't a pilot. He was a radio operator and a waist gunner. He never ran the show, but he knew what his part was and he wanted that show to begin.

Impatience is something we learned very fast, my brother and I, growing up. We learned to hate red lights, slow talkers, and people standing in front of us. My mother was the only calm one in the family. But since she died very young, her legacy of meekness and forbearance was eclipsed almost instantly by my father's unwillingness to suffer fools gladly. Anybody outside the family was a fool. Pretty much anybody inside the family was one, too.

I thought I'd get away with never having to learn patience myself. Even now, when my students tell me I speak too fast during my lectures, I tell them life is short, listen faster. Secretly, I always felt as if I'd escaped the need to learn patience because I'd avoided having kids. Although I helped raise my two stepsons, I met them when they were young teenagers. They required understanding, a sense of humor, and money for gas. Not having an infant meant I never developed the gentle, self-possessed poise that's necessary to help a child learn to speak, learn to walk, and learn to enter the world. I skipped that part.

But during my father's illness I learned that the noun "patient" and the adjective "patient" are—no surprise—not merely etymologically bred from the same root (the Latin present participle *pati*, to suffer): they also hold within them the seeds of what's necessary when dealing with death. When someone you love is a patient, meaning that he is suffering, enduring pain, indignity, and helplessness, the only thing that you can do is find patience in yourself.

Curled like a claw in his hospital bed, unable to move and barely able to speak, I remember a look in my father's eyes like the one from those photographs of him at nineteen during the war. My father, forever the New Yorker, was always thinking, "C'mon already. I don't have all day."

And one day, finally, he didn't.

59

The Hummingbird Effect

Sometimes it's not enough to be focused—sometimes you need to accept help and sometimes you need to be flexible.

Once a ruby-throated hummingbird, which had flown more than 2,000 miles from Central America just to get to our neighborhood, got stuck in our garage. He panicked and couldn't find his way out.

(Caveat lector: I'm going to anthropomorphize the hell out of this hummingbird. I thought you should be made aware of this the way IMDB makes you aware that certain synopses contain "spoilers.")

Panic makes you lose your bearings and obliterates any view of your ultimate destination. You retain only a flickering awareness of reality. Feeling trapped and scared makes you as lightheaded as someone breathing ether or drinking ethanol.

When you're frantic, you'll do anything just to do something.

The urgency of chaos sends even instinct out the window—or crashes against its glass.

Careening wildly into the walls, the meticulously beautiful creature couldn't draw on skills that permitted him to fly directly over the Gulf of Mexico or maneuver up, down, backward, and forward as he sipped his body weight in sugar water and nectar every day.

I improvised with a broom and my husband found a net. With small gestures, we encouraged the hummingbird to stop hitting his head against the ceiling. Finally, his extraordinarily tiny claws clasped the net and Michael deftly stepped outside. After maybe two seconds of complete stillness, the bird flew off in a straight line into the treetops and disappeared.

Although the episode ended happily, I'm sure the hummingbird is telling some tall tales to his avian companions.

You'll say I'm projecting and you'll be right. Not only do I sympathize with ingesting my own body weight, I also recognized the bird's desperation. You see, I've spent time, especially in my earlier years, as a subject of panic attacks.

Notice I say "a subject of" and not "subject to": I felt as if I was their slave and I lived in an unsteady world over which they—the panic attacks—ruled.

As a child I was afraid to walk over grates (fear of falling through), afraid of subway cars running on parallel tracks (fear they would collide), and of dogs (fear of being torn to pieces).

My most "normal" childhood fear, fear of being abandoned by my parents, was the only one that came true: my mother died when I was still in high school.

I became afraid that I hadn't worried enough, and my panic attacks became worse.

I was terrified—not just worried by but terrified—of phone calls or letters that weren't answered immediately (fear that the person who was meant to respond had died) and planes (would I live to return home; would I want to return home?).

I wrecked relationships because I was afraid of ruining them.

I would try to reach people—not only boyfriends but also relatives and acquaintances—obsessively making contact until I could speak to them. Remember, this was before answering machines and computers; information passed more slowly, although that doesn't explain my behavior.

There was, for example, a faraway aunt who was one of my mother's lesser sisters. When, after not speaking to her for months, I couldn't get her on the phone one day, I was certain she'd died. I went to the library to find the number for my cousin, who lived in a distant city, and called him, weeping. I unnerved him. Of course she was fine. Eventually it turned into one of those funny family stories. Eventually.

When I was in the middle of it, though, I felt like I was smashing against the corners of an unfamiliar room. And I was afraid of people coming for me with a net, even if they looked benevolent. Would the safety net tighten into a snare?

It's not surprising that an inexplicably weeping, shivering, frantic girl drove many good-hearted people away. Nevertheless, there were others who persuaded me to accept help. Focused only on fear, I saw only blank walls. They offered their own methods of extraction.

I learned to see clear skies and a way out, grateful to replace the exhausting and compulsive need to flee with an invigorating and resilient passion for flight.

PART 7

Seeing Something,

Saying Something

60

If You Lean In, Will Men Just Look Down Your Blouse?

Imagine hearing the phrase: "Wow, you're just like one of the guys!"

Then imagine hearing the phrase: "Wow, you're just like every other woman!"

Now decide which phrase is a compliment.

That didn't take very long, did it? "Just like one of the guys" is usually high praise indeed. For most girls and women, it implies she's independent, trustworthy, candid, and fair-minded and understands what it means to "code" (or at least get in touch with someone who does).

"Just like one of the guys" means she can throw fast and speak up, where, in contrast, the "acting like a girl" means she can speak fast and throw up.

Even for girls who never wanted to be a boy and never envied their brothers, or those who grew up in rare households where the phrase "gender equity" was thrown around as casually as "pass the salt," the cultural association of masculinity with freedom, independence, and the ability to choose one's own destiny without interference from biology (now often translated into the apparently benign and yet treacherous work/life balance mantra, espoused by those who reject the term "feminist" in favor of the term "humanist"), remains the blueprint for twenty-first-century America.

It's impossible to escape the fact of masculine privilege. For those who identify with men, they see this cornerstone as a building block rather than a stumbling block. Like Ann Coulter, Sarah Palin, or the Rules Girls, they escape the straitjacket of conventional femininity while lacing the stays on their sisters more tightly.

Even if you grew up in a house free of Barbies or devoid of Disney movies, no one can be raised in a vacuum. It's like being allergic to houseplants or pets: Your own home can be free of cats, dogs, or philodendrons, but at a certain point you have to step outside. You can't escape the atmosphere. You breathe it in, like pollen.

Isn't it odd that only a rare woman wants to hear herself compared to a member of her own sex, as if it's an insult beyond reconciliation? "Don't call me 'woman,'" snaps a character from one of Dorothy Parker's stories, to which her paramour replies, "I'm sorry, darling, I didn't mean to use bad words."

We have internalized the idea of what I see as a kind of "Female Exceptionalism" so entirely that we don't even notice it anymore. A smart, capable, alert, and confident girl or young woman will often, whether by her family, by her teachers, or by her bosses, be told that she belongs to the small elite group who are not like other members of her sex. This is meant—and is usually accepted—as an accolade.

For all the "Grrl Power" videos and songs, I'm not convinced much has changed since I was a teenager. Conspicuous as my Love's Baby Soft perfume and twice as irritating, my scorn for other girls was unmistakable. They were getting beauty tips from *Seventeen* magazine while I was singing along to "At Seventeen;" they were bopping along to "Love Will Keep Us Together" while

I was reading *Looking for Mr. Goodbar,* a literary novel about a woman's desperation.

Growing up, I had eyebrow-raised contempt for those lesser creatures who spent all their time perfecting lip gloss and curling their hair—at least, I had contempt for the girls doing this. The cross-dressing guys in my school were far better at it. That's one reason I maintain, to this day, the only ones who are happy to hear "You're just like a woman!" are contestants on *RuPaul's Drag Race.*

Forty years later, smart, hip female students queue up outside my office by the dozen to talk about how their best friends are male, how all the women they meet want to discuss only what's trivial, and how their friends are bopping along to Taylor Swift while they're reading *Gone Girl,* a literary novel about a woman's desperation.

They repeat the catechism I used with few alterations: "All my best friends are guys. Guys just get me, you know? It's not a sexual thing; we're just friends. I have a boyfriend, but he doesn't actually even hang out with my guy friends. But I can only really talk to my male friends because other girls are just, like, too jealous and weird and competitive."

When I suggest that they connect with the other twenty-three women loitering in the hallway who feel precisely the same way, they shrug it off. They think I don't get it.

But I get it: like them, I longed for the imprimatur of masculine approval. My immediate family consisted of a father and a brother; I attended what had been an all-male college; I was promoted to full professor before menopause. I know what it's like to live in Guy World and be encouraged to seek the tiara of the Woman Who Is Unlike Others.

How are we taught this? By the scene in Jane Austen novels where you learn to recognize the heroine because she is distinct and placed above her shallow, insignificant sisters. By the scene in every romantic comedy where the charming hero gazes at the female protagonist in wonderment and murmurs, "I don't believe there's another woman like you in the whole world." By the fact that entry into a "man's world" remains a ticket to what's considered the "real world" or "professional world," as if women are not quite people and are always amateurs.

In her short story "Man from Mars," Margaret Atwood describes such a woman: "[S]he even had a kind of special position among men: she was an exception, she fitted none of the categories they commonly used when talking about girls: she wasn't a cock-teaser, a cold fish, an easy lay, or a snarky bitch; she was an honorary person. She had grown to share their contempt for most women."

Here's the question: Can a woman run with the big dogs and avoid being thought of as a bitch? Not until women stop pretending to be what we aren't and cross-acting (if not cross-dressing) as guys.

Until the reaction to hearing "You're just like a woman" is "You mean I'm clever, creative, dynamic, and empathetic? Thanks!" we still have work to do.

Women are still working on getting hold of the map, or the keys, or at least the GPS coordinates to our most deeply cherished dreams. While multimillionaire Sheryl Sandberg's slim volume, *Lean In,* seems to be offering a Google Earth picture of where women want to be—a place where men share parenting and homemaking responsibilities equally with their female partners, where gender-balanced workplaces are unremarkable, and where, by age forty-three, you're worth hundreds of millions of dollars and running a couple of Fortune 500 companies—I think Sandberg's offering more of a mirage than a map.

Sure, it sounds lovely: a place where Glinda the Good Witch not only wears Prada but also is COO of Prada and hires her green sister to work in human resources because women have to learn to work together. And I sure do appreciate that Sandberg uses the *f* word—"feminist"—to describe her work and her perspective; "feminist" is still the most intimidating *f* word in America. Lots of young women avoid the *f* word. I've had female students trip all over themselves to avoid using it: "I'm getting a doctoral fellowship from NASA after I complete my NEA grant, although I hope it's the work I did for girls in Tanzania in the Peace Corps that'll be my legacy. But I'm not a feminist. I like lipstick and want to get married one day." They fear feminism is about wearing your hair in braids and yelling slogans blaming men for stuff.

(There are six women in Berkeley still doing this. They're fabulous and I'm grateful to them for getting the whole thing going.)

I've argued that feminism is the belief that women are human beings. I simply assume everybody I meet—men and women alike—is a feminist because I give people the benefit of the doubt. You're using cutlery? You don't wear T-shirts saying "Men: no shirt, no service; Women: no shirt, free drinks!"? You don't think women are just a man's way of making more men? Then, honey, you're a feminist.

It's my version of feminism, which is sort of like a hip nun's version of Catholicism—affirming to all and not guided by rulebooks or doctrinal declarations—that makes me uncertain whether to applaud or denounce the ruckus going on within what is unnervingly called the Mommy War. I always start by explaining that I've never raised young children. I have two terrific stepsons—now at that absolutely *adorable* age where they are attorneys—and that's why I rarely weigh in on motherhood discussions. I'm not a card-carrying member; mine is a proxy vote.

Yet what gets me is this: Why do women feel unqualified to comment on subjects beyond those we know firsthand—as I do when talking about raising children? Ever notice the number of experts on women's issues and motherhood—not just parenting, but motherhood—who seem to be men? They're not apologizing for not having firsthand experience. Women waste a whole lot of precious time trying to judge ourselves and evaluate our worth. We have to stop competing with other women, as if women who make other choices in their lives are our adversaries.

Checking to see if you're better or worse than other women is the moral and ethical version of trying to catch a glimpse of yourself unawares in a storefront window; it hardly ever works. The view is always distorted.

Current cultural clichés insist today's woman is either trying on negligees while having the nanny deal with the triplets or else having her bunions shaved, the ones caused by wearing steel-toed, hardworking shoes.

It's not that easy.

At certain moments, Sandberg sounds as if she doesn't understand how nickeled-and-dimed women really live and work. She sounds a little like an ace pilot giving a pep talk to baggage handlers. If you've never been on a plane, it's a little hard to feel the wind under your wings—especially when you're handling valuable goods ultimately going to other people.

When Sandberg talks about "forcing" herself to leave the office at 5:30 so she could go home and have dinner with her kids, for example—because otherwise her new job would prove "unsustainable"—I'm thinking about those friends of mine who work as sous-chefs, taxi dispatchers, and sales associates. What if they told their bosses their work/life balance would become "unsustainable" if they didn't leave earlier than everybody else?

I doubt their employers would have employed the language of Mark Zuckerberg. Sandberg's boss cheers his colleague for having "an extremely high IQ and EQ," thus praising both her brains and her emotional acumen.

When I asked the taxi dispatcher whether her EQ came into play at work, her reply was as follows: "If I even said the term 'EQ' to one of these guys, their immediate response would be, 'Yeah? Well, EQ too.'"

What did she think about *Lean In?*

"At my job, if I lean in, guys just look down my blouse."

For many of us, reading books about wildly high-profile women is a form of masochism. It's like tearing off your cuticles. We turn pages and wonder, "Why can't I be more like her?"

Then we think what we could have done better.

If only we'd been more focused as teenagers. (That probably would have been possible.) And if only we'd done our senior thesis at Harvard with Larry Summers, who'd have coached us to get our MBA at Harvard and then hired us at twenty-nine to become chief of staff at the Treasury Department. (Maybe slightly less possible.)

I'm just saying that not everybody has access to the same playing field as Sandberg and that point needs to be recognized.

Some people are still on the public bus trying to get to the field where the game is being played; it takes a longer time if you have to transfer from one route to another.

The lives of all adult human beings are awkward, messy, and full of glandular issues. As human beings, women are no exception. Yet we keep thinking we should be; we keep thinking we are not included in "all adult human beings" but must be separated into increasingly smaller categories.

But until every woman has access to employment at wages equal to her male colleagues, until women are not told, as Microsoft CEO Satya Nadella announced at the Grace Hopper Celebration of Women in Computing, that women should trust "the system" and rely on "karma" to reward them financially and not ask for raises (as if that's worked really well up to now), and until every child has a stable secure home, everything else sidesteps the real issue of equity.

61

Good Girls Say No—and Women Should, Too

A good girl is defined as one who almost always says "No." A good woman is defined as one who almost always says "Yes."

Allow me to clarify: the tasks each group is being asked to perform are rarely the same.

To be a good girl one must say no when boys with pickup trucks ask to go for rides in the country. A good girl says no if asked, whether it's by the brother of her best friend, her math teacher, or the circus, to run away. One must also say no when a decidedly flirtatious and overly eager adult offers to pay for one's education if one promises to accompany said adult to Italy once the education has been duly completed; besides, that only happens in Edwardian novels.

Why?

Just as a good girl is encouraged to say no automatically, having been instructed that sex is filthy and degrading and must be saved for her true love, a good woman says yes to do everything before she knows it because she has been encouraged to believe that only by being agreeable and complacent will she be valued and liked.

We agree to sell raffle tickets before the information hits the actual thinking lobes of our brains. Why else would anyone agree to walk around with a four-pound roll of colored paper hitting people up for small sums of money at an otherwise (possibly) fun event?

I sold raffle tickets once. With God as my witness, I will never do it again. Other mistakes I am bound to repeat, but not this one. Because I was too embarrassed to keep going from table to table like an inspector from the USDA, I spent more than 250 bucks. I still didn't win the cellophane-clad basket filled with what looked like cheese graters, balsamic vinegar, nutcrackers, and dice (hey, maybe it was nougat, but to me they looked as if they should be rolled on a green felt table).

Good women will agree to serve dinner for twenty-six at the holidays—including four gluten-free, three vegan, two lactose-intolerant guests. And a person on a diet who brings microwavable protein curds—simply to get pleading people to stop asking us for favors in that horrible wheedling voice.

There's a voice both women and men will use when asking favors of women that would never be used when asking a favor of a man.

Here's an example: I got a message asking me to "Give a talk to an all-female management team about the importance of negotiation in asking for pay-raises."

Maybe the large company requesting my presence actually wanted its female employees to learn how to present their skills most effectively when asking for advancement. Hey, anything is possible.

Yet the woman inviting me to speak, who worked in human resources, saw no irony in explaining to me that the invitation would include lunch but not offer any sort of honorarium.

Isn't that like saying, "We want you to teach an assertiveness training class and we insist you do it exactly on our terms"?

Put it this way: is it really helping women generally if we tell women individually that their work isn't worth what they're asking?

Before giving an answer, I asked other women about whether they'd had similar experiences. I had no idea there would be such a chorus, and such a diverse chorus at that. I heard from three female clergy members. I heard from a number of nurses and physicians who felt perpetually on-call.

Women writers, singers, musicians, and artists (especially photographers) expressed their frustration at being asked to give, often at a cost to themselves, their time and talent for everything from gala fund-raisers (at least one's work gets attention plus it's for a good cause) to bridal showers of friends who'd been out of touch for years (not as unselfish an invite).

I heard from a disgruntled scrapbooker.

A newly minted divorce attorney who initially offered a sliding scale when dealing with clients explained: "My largesse has led to my feeling abused. It seems that when you don't bill you give the green light for texts and phone calls at all hours of the day and night. . . . These same clients . . . most definitely play the gender card. There is a presumption that as a woman I am deeply invested in their individual situations . . . and that I should work free of charge."

Yet I have hope, as always, for the future.

In her mid-twenties, Caitlin, assistant to the president at a New England college understands that saying yes to as many professional opportunities as possible is crucial because young workers "need to get experience." But Caitlin also knows that saying, "No, thanks," or, "That's not appropriate for my role" is equally important—if, for example, you're asked to drive someone you've never met home from a university event. She has "been rewarded with raises and a promotion" which is more useful than a wink and a pat on the head.

What's most specious about being asked to work for less or work for free is that it's almost always women who are sent to do the asking. They wouldn't let a guy do it because it would seem sexist and demeaning.

Why? Because it is sexist and demeaning.

And that's why I explained, in gentle but certain terms, that my fee was non-negotiable. That's not because I'm ungenerous or inflexible but because this hypocritical gender provincialism isn't helping any of us: in such ways do women become complicitous in our own undoing.

If you were asking, say, Don Draper from *Mad Men* for a lift to the airport, would you use a wheedling voice? No, you wouldn't. In fact, you'd use your voice to call a cab because you would never ask Don Draper to take you to the airport because you know he's busy. But you'd ask Peggy, wouldn't you, even though she's as smart as Don? And you'd plead your case, telling her—wheedling slightly in a Pete Campbell sort of way even though you'd despise yourself for it—that only she could be trusted to be there on time because she'd know how scared you were of flying?

I've done that. Not to Peggy (or even brilliant Elisabeth Moss, who played her), but to her counterparts in my life. Sure, I've returned the favor, driving them to places that scared them or back from places they hated to leave.

But I'd also pick Don up, you see, even though he'd never be there for me.

And that's what makes good women feel, all too often, like fools. Maybe girls don't need to learn to say yes more often—just watch one episode of *Teen Mom*—but many women need to relearn to say no.

Just as good girls get knocked up because bad girls know better, good women are exploited, taken for granted, overrun by the needs of others, and treated as if they matter only when they're putting themselves aside.

"Say yes only when you mean it": wise advice at any age.

62

Why We Know That When Guys Make Slurping Sounds at Us on the Street, It Isn't a Compliment

Yes, all women, all girls, grow up learning ways to avoid attracting the attention of unnerving guys; it's no doubt built into our DNA, along with an affection for miniatures and the early songs of Patsy Cline.

Simply in order to leave the house in the morning, a girl has to assemble an arsenal of behaviors to just "shut that whole thing down." You remember that phrase, right? That was a gem from Todd Akin, R-MO, who argued that women don't get pregnant from criminal acts because "[i]f it's a legitimate rape, the female body has ways to try to shut that whole thing down."

I'm not saying that getting harassed on the street is even close to being in the same category as getting raped, but I am saying the ignorant assumption behind Akin's remark—that women's bodies are responsible for everything that happens to us—is part of a continuum.

This insidious sense we use to protect ourselves against what damage we can bring upon ourselves begins very early.

Every girl remembers the first time she was degraded sexually in public. It is not, as the movies would have us believe, a wonderfully cheerful moment of sensual awakening and blossoming womanhood.

It's the moment when you start carrying your keys in your hand so you've got quick access to the door plus some metal between your fingers, and when you should have your phone pre-dialed to 911, so that there's only one more button to hit.

It's the sense of shame sweeping over you because you looked "pretty"— only to be slimed in a drive-by insult, and told you look like a hooker. It's knowing where the well-lit streets are because you are afraid of the dark, and it's being wary of the spotlight because if you're the center of attention you're an easy target.

It's developing a ninja-like awareness of your surroundings even when you're supposed to be relaxed and enjoying yourself. It's recognizing that nowhere is safe.

If girls standing on the lawn of the California house back in a college town in 2014 weren't safe from a twenty-two-year-old who wanted to prove he was the "alpha man" by slaughtering them, then nowhere is safe.

We develop strategies to make ourselves feel, if not safe, then safer. They are talismanic rather than scientific, but some do work.

I discovered around age twelve, for example, that one way to dissuade men from leering at me or making sucking-teeth-clicking noises as I passed them on the street was to stick a finger in my ear and start digging. You have to look really determined; you have to appear on a mission.

It can't look like you're twirling a strand of your hair or something like that, because that might be seen as cute and then you couldn't expect anybody's sympathy even if you were abducted and forced to live on a farm with Todd Akin.

If that didn't work and an intimidating presence remained nearby—let's say on a subway or bus where you couldn't just sneak away casually but had to stay in your seat for fear of never finding one again—sticking another finger unapologetically and directly into a nostril and keeping it there would, nine times out of ten, work instantly.

That you'd never be able to get a date in that borough with a normal guy would be the downside.

Yes, all women and girls have ways of making ourselves inconspicuous. It isn't modesty that drives us to do it: It's fear. It's self-protection. And don't tell yourself we're being forced into the virtue of modesty, because we're not, no more than a man with his hand cut off is being forced into the virtue of patience.

It's also hard to get ahead in the world if you spend a lot of time looking over your shoulder to make sure you're not being stalked.

Yet, yes, all women want love. But what disguises itself under that name, smuggled in under a fake passport? You know that somewhere there's a teenage girl feeling really bad for the Santa Barbara murderer because "all he needed was somebody to love him." She's writing poems to him right now, romanticizing the violence and turning pathology into romance.

And yes, while all people wish we could shut it all out and pretend it will all go away, we can't. Hatred, disguised as lust, haunts, corrodes, and seeps from one generation to the next.

The system that supports it can't be ignored; it must be dismantled. It's work that needs to be done by us—by all of us.

63

Never Mind Mindfulness

I'm pretty much done with mindfulness. I'm just going to start paying attention. Detachment is now as overrated as quinoa and just about as inspiring.

Mindfulness has become, at least for the non-practicing Buddhists among us, an often-convenient excuse for shirking the hard work of making decisions and shrugging off life's emotional bill.

As I understand it, mindfulness is the cultivation of an evenly hovering experience of present awareness, which means being open and receptive to everything without passing judgment or reacting reflexively.

Personally, I stopped paying attention to that definition after the ninth word.

And yet I'm somebody who's pretty good at paying attention.

I cut my teeth on the phrase "Pay attention, kid, and you just might learn something," because the person saying it was usually right: I learned something by watching or listening and was then able to imitate or avoid whatever they were doing.

You paid attention to your grandmother in the kitchen and learned to make *spittini* so perfect you still never order them even in a five-star restaurant because the ones you make at home are better.

You paid attention when the cousin who wore too much eyeliner and thought girls should let boys win got married in a tent dress, then had a baby seven months later. You decided to put your hand up in class and shout out the right answers even if the teacher, who also thought girls should let boys win, wouldn't call on you.

You learned to make decisions, judgments, and choices. You joined the world's conversation, which meant being informed and speaking out.

You learned to take sides, even when you could see the valid points made by the opposition. You developed opinions and embraced beliefs because you discovered that news, history, and institutions, formed by those in power, shaped both culture and environment and did not merely reflect them.

You want more than to be "in" the moment because being "in" it isn't enough. You want to throw your arms around it and hold on to it, wringing every bit of intensity, significance, and pleasure from the moment the way you'd wring water out of a wet cloth.

It's impossible, of course: every moment, like water, evades, slips away, turns into something else.

As Heraclitus (a friend from the old neighborhood) used to say, no one can ever step in the same river twice.

But that doesn't mean you shouldn't want to make a splash, or immerse yourself entirely, or soak it all up.

It's true that mindfulness keeps the surface tension unbroken and calm; in its unwillingness to choose and its inability to commit it certainly does keep its options open.

But this tidy sense of disengagement comes at a great cost: one forgoes passion, fascination, and an urgent sense of purposefulness in order to preserve inwardly focused self-regulation.

Paying attention is hard work. It's like putting pressure on a wound—you can't let up or it starts bleeding again, but you know there's blood in your veins. Not only will it keep you alive; it will also help you deal with others who have been wounded.

In many ways, mindfulness and detachment have taken the place of multitasking, or perhaps they're multitasking's offspring. If you do everything simultaneously and without pausing, trying always to see the big picture without focusing on any one thing, the likelihood of creating something, grasping a new idea, or initiating something of consequence thins out, like pastry rolled too fine, to the point where its integrity is diminished.

Multitasking was whole grain; mindfulness is a smoothie.

Do you really want to make all of life's experiences into a smoothie?

Do you really want to blend it all into a cleansing mixture that you can have alone, without the mess of human interaction? By throwing everything in together, even if it's healthy, don't you remove the texture and flatten the taste? There's no crispness or crunch, no warm center or surprising sudden spice. You might as well take time by injection, removing the piquancy of fun, loyalty, and intensity altogether.

Surely we were given our brief lives for more than a walk through the world with a "Do Not Disturb" sign hanging from our necks?

64

A Good Eater's Guide to Actual Food

1. Strawberries should be the size of your thumbnail and not the size of a Spaldeen. A strawberry as big as a rubber ball will taste like a rubber ball.

2. Have you noticed that we live in a nation where special interest groups will defend the carrying of AR-15s into public spaces while a person carrying a concealed bag of peanuts onto an airplane will be placed on the "No Fly" List?

3. Kale is overrated. Don't kid yourself. It's a fad. The next thing they're going to be telling us to eat is plankton, and they'll be telling us to sieve it through our teeth like whales.

4. "Sustainability" is not another word for "deliciousness." Most things that are delicious in life can be scooped—think ice cream, mashed potatoes, macaroni and cheese, coleslaw, stuffing, and butter. (NB: the scoop for butter is usually smaller but not always.)

5. Speaking of butter, even *Time* magazine put it on the front cover. Butter is always the secret ingredient. You can sauté something in

butter, along with garlic, salt, and pepper, and it will be delicious. This includes snails, old sneakers, sheep's eyeballs, and, perhaps, kale.

6. Cheese.

7. "Homemade," like "sustainable," does not guarantee delicious. Have you ever seen some people's homes? Have you visited their kitchens? Do you really want to eat stuff made there? The same goes for "made with love." Have you seen some people's love? Do you want that to be a main ingredient? Remember: there's a reason analysts call some relationships toxic.

8. "Grilled," like "sustainable" or "homemade," does not always guarantee delicious. Although some folks know what they are doing, some people just pour half a can of lighter fluid into a metal container, which happens to be on their decks, and they are not exactly master chefs. They might just be nascent pyromaniacs who found strip steak on sale. It might be good to bring along some potato salad just in case. Potato salad can be scooped.

9. Beware the midsummer picnic if it relies heavily on mayonnaise-based dishes. On a 110-degree day, chicken salad, shrimp salad, potato salad, and egg salad can kill you outright. Once they've been uncovered for more than thirty-five seconds, even the fact that they've been scooped doesn't matter. While it's true that the flies and other insects that land in the serving dishes will add protein, some people don't appreciate their exoskeleton crunchiness.

10. Rhubarb, while nice in a pie when mixed with small strawberries, should not be used instead of a floral centerpiece. Nor should it be presented as a bouquet, however decorative it seems when eyed at the Farmer's Market. Don't even think about using rhubarb in a corsage.

11. Not all desserts are created equal. Whipped yogurt is not ice cream. Frozen yogurt is not ice cream. Yogurt shaped into ice cream bars is not ice cream. If you are someone who serves any version of this on top of an actual dessert item and asks your guests whether they can tell the difference, they will say they can't. Be assured that they are merely being polite.

12. "Skinny" should never be used to describe anything appealing. Think of a "skinny dog" or a "skinny baby." Not appealing, right? A little unnerving, to be honest. "Skinny," when the world was sane, used to mean "underfed and malnourished," which translated to "unhappy, grasping, and needy." A truly "skinny martini" is a bottle of cheap grain alcohol and a straw.

13. If you like anchovies, forging a lifetime partnership, be it professional or personal, with someone else who likes anchovies is useful—you will always be able to split the Caesar salad and order pizza with no apologies or explanations.

14. Sitting next to someone during a meal who says, "That's not really good for you," or, "Do you really need that?" is worse for your health than a corned-beef sandwich, two pounds of curly fries, a piece of blackout cake, and a double espresso.

15. More cheese.

65

Please Don't Eat the Placentas!

I have to stop reading New York magazine.

Most of the time I regard magazines as a treat. I read them when I'm taking a bath, when I'm traveling, or when I'm having a meal alone. They're the potato chips of my reading life: I can grab a handful, feel a twinge of self-indulgence, and yet feel good about not destroying my appetite for more serious stuff.

But reading an article titled "The Placenta Cookbook" in *New York* explaining how "[f]or a growing number of new mothers, there's no better nutritional snack after childbirth than the fruit of their own labors"—literally—I sort of lost my appetite for, well, almost everything.

Here's an excerpt—and tell me it doesn't make you think of Swift's Modest Proposal—which sounds exactly like some anti-feminist parody off a creepy woman-hating website: "A few years ago, a group of mothers organized a placenta picnic in Prospect Park where they compared placenta-eating experiences, and considered performing a mass burial of leftover parts they had kept. Loretta Jordan, a Bronx-based doula who organized the picnic, would go on to drink a piece of her daughter's placenta in a 'top-shelf Bloody Mary.' "

After thinking of Swift, the next person I thought of was good old Jean Kerr, author of *Please Don't Eat the Daisies*.

The premise of the essay titled "Please Don't Eat the Daisies" is that you have to tell kids what not to do: "don't tease the dog," "don't torture your younger brother," "don't put the turtles in the refrigerator to see what would happen to them in cold climates." The poor beleaguered parent, however, neglects to tell them not to eat the floral arrangement, having not imagined that any sane person of any age would do such a thing, and discovers upon her return home that, of course, the children have devoured the flowers, petals and all.

Insert gentle, domestic laughter here.

And, sure, cosmetic companies have advertised "placenta products" for years. You slap it around your eyes for a hundred bucks a pop and it'll make you look like you were born yesterday—instead of just spending money as if you were.

Placenta eating, though—really? Is this where sixty years of the women's rights movement has brought us? To a kitchen where some poor woman is cooking a rich woman's afterbirth and making it into pills or jerky or some other kind of more palatable foodstuff so that the fancier woman can—taking narcissism to new heights—consume herself?

66

Words Rich People Use That Poor People Don't

According to an article in *The New York Times*, poor people need to read to their children because, "by age 3, the children of wealthier professionals have heard words millions more times than have those of less educated, low-income parents, giving the children who have heard more words a distinct advantage in school."

Is this a surprise to anybody?

I mean, are we actually shocked to discover that American children from families with high incomes are read to daily from birth to five years of age, compared with around a third of children from families living below the poverty line?

Are we gasping in surprise to learn that "affluent children had learned 30 percent more words . . . than children from low-income homes"? I don't think so.

If you're living below the poverty line, you don't have a whole lot of time to read to your kids. This is because, if you're living below the poverty line, you are trying to feed your kids, trying to keep your kids clean and healthy, and probably trying desperately to move to a neighborhood where your kids are not likely to be shot, stabbed, or thrown out a window by drug dealers.

I teach reading and writing for a living; it's not that I don't know the importance of books and language. I support literacy at any age and under any circumstances; I've done fund-raisers for early literacy programs and believe that the sooner everybody gets a book in his or her hands, the better off we'll all be.

And I was raised in a poor family, so I get that part of it, too. Sometimes my parents read to us, sure. But often they were way too tired and simply fell asleep on the bed next to my brother and me between the first and second page of *The Poky Little Puppy*. They worked all the time, remember?

That didn't allow my poor parents massive amounts of leisure or even actual conscious time during which they could pick up, say, *Winnie-the-Pooh* and explain while reading the classic children's work that Christopher Robin wasn't wearing blue braces on his teeth but that braces are what the British call suspenders—even if they knew that, which they wouldn't have, because how would they have known such a thing themselves?

There are *big* class differences in America. We don't like to talk about them. (We certainly don't like to talk about race and wouldn't like to say about the picture illustrating the article in *The Times*, "Hmm, there's a white doctor next to a black woman with her child, and the white doctor is holding a book as if to say, 'See how this is done?'")

There are lots of terms underprivileged tots don't know as well as their upper-class counterparts and I'm not sure reading to them—as important as it is—will truly close the gap. How about giving their parents more access to well-paying, stable jobs?

But if we were going to talk about some of the specific words that those children of wealthier professionals have heard millions more times than the poor kids have heard—if we really wanted to make the list detailed—that list might include the following vocabulary terms marking the differences between rich kids and the poor kids:

Amenities

- "amuse-bouche"
- "antiquarian"
- "archivist"
- "Aspen"
- "Aubusson rug"
- "au pair"
- "Baccarat crystal"
- "board of directors"
- "calligraphy"
- "Canyon Ranch"
- "chaise longue"
- "chèvre"
- "Chilean Seabass"
- "commodity strategies"
- "conservatory"
- "cotillion"
- "coxswain"
- "dermatologist"
- "docent"
- "entrepreneurship"
- "equestrian program"
- "escrow"
- "facilitator"
- "first-edition"
- "gap year"
- "grandfather's canoe"
- "heirloom tomato"
- "Hermès"
- "iambic"
- "juice cleanse"
- "kale"
- "lacrosse"
- "the longer back nine"
- "mudroom"
- "Nice"
- "orthodontist"
- "palate cleanser"
- "personal trainer"
- "pooled investment vehicle"
- "private wealth management"
- "Quentin Crisp"
- "ramekin"
- "regatta"
- "sommelier"
- "summer" or "winter" as verbs
- "tartan"
- "tax-free municipal bonds"
- "tennis camp"
- "thread count"
- "unpaid internship"
- "valet"
- "Viscount"
- "Wellingtons"
- "yoga"
- "Zendesk"

Not that I'm bitter, but it's not about reading *The Poky Little Puppy*. It's about acknowledging and altering the poky little inequalities in terms of financial, economic, educational, class, and gender divides in this country.

It's about privilege and the lack of it—and it's about addressing the underlying causes of poverty.

67

A Proactive, Impactful Look at Words I Despise

Although I love language, there are certain words that make me break out in hives. I have an allergic reaction when I see or hear them: I shiver as my temperature rises, I turn a mottled shade somewhere between mauve and crimson and my jaw clamps shut.

Like poison ivy, these often appear in clumps. Most recently, I've walked into thickets and groves of the following toxic terms: "disrupt," "cohort," "synergy," "lifestyle," "wheelhouse," "iconic," "branding," "curated," "vocalize," "artisanal," "impactful," and "relatable."

"Toxic" should probably be there, too.

What's wrong with these words? Individually and in their native habitats, they're fine. "Vocalize" is dandy, fitting snugly into the world of music; as my friend Jana explains, " 'Vocalize' should be restricted only to use by singers, who associate very specific meanings and actions to the word." She goes on to ask, "What term is the corporate world going to appropriate next—'audiate'?"

But when my students write: "Jane Eyre vocalized her inner emotions to Mr. Rochester" I underline "vocalized" as well as "inner emotions" and insist they write something more text-specific, precise, and informative. "What do you mean and why is it important?" is what I usually ask.

By the third rewrite, they usually know what they mean and they know how to say it.

I've learned, after twenty-eight years of teaching, that "vocalize," like "relatable," is a dodge: it is an intellectual sleight of hand. If a student defines a character as "relatable," I ask, "Does that mean he's sympathetic, intriguing, recognizable, emotionally complex, clichéd, seductive, likable, familiar, accessible, or perspicuous?" If my student says, "Yeah, that's right—relatable," I know she hasn't done any of the reading.

Overused or misused words become bankrupted of whatever original meanings they might have had. Used to obscure rather than to clarify ideas, they don't express thought but instead divert attention away from the fact that the person using the term employs it as an act of camouflage, disguising his or her inability to say what needs saying.

"Proactive," for example, should be struck from our vocabulary.

Why? Because it means "active." A friend, who knows that "proactive" is anathema to me, said, "I want to motivate my staff. I tell them to be 'proactive.' What other words can I use?"

"How about asking them to be enthusiastic, energetic, engaged, insightful, or thoughtful? Even better, how about asking them to do what you really want? You want their focused attention? Ask for it. You want them to tell you practical ways in which they can do their jobs better? Make it possible for them to be direct and honest in their responses and then make the changes they suggest."

You don't have to "implement" "fundamental paradigm shifts" as an "influencer" to "ensure sustainable best practices" by "mobilizing your resources" in an "accelerated," "idea-driven," and "powerfully transformative" "watershed event" with "high-stakes," "holistic" "modeling behavior" creating an "organic," "abundant," and "quantifiably," if not "dazzling," "win-win" environment that will be so "mindful" and "balanced" that "gurus" and "unicorns" from throughout the "blogosphere" will applaud the "mission and mandate" your "revolutionizing vision" will have on "setting a gold standard."

Next in line for execution (as in "to be exterminated" not as in "being put to use") are feeble conversational caveats such as "I just wanted to say," "No offense, but," "Can I just mention that," and "I don't know if you'd agree, but . . ."

When folks begin sentences this way I want to shout, "If you're going to say something dull, uninformed, or belligerent, don't apologize in advance. Either stand up for what's coming out of your mouth or wait until you know what you think before you speak."

Also deserving to be driven out of our vocabularies with pitchforks and torches are the following: "moving forward," "circle back," "content-driven," "low-hanging fruit," "hashtagging," "out of the box," "thought leader," "takeaway," and "come together." (Of this last one, my friend Rose Valenta quips, "Are we all practicing our Kegel exercises now?")

Of course the "ize" have it: "optimize," "monetize," "galvanize," "strategize," "prioritize," "incentivize," "globalize," and "utilize."

Why use "utilize" when you can use "use"?

If you love language, treat it with respect, honor, and intimacy. Play with it, but never treat it lightly.

And never, ever use the word "impactful."

68

Moments of the Irrevocable

The world will be different by tomorrow morning.

Sure, every week, every day, every moment, the world changes. Not only in the big ways, either; not only because within the passage of a second, within the length of a heartbeat, someone is born and someone dies. There are pivotal moments in life between these two junctures, smaller but perhaps as providential.

As I struggle to give myself permission to write, there are young people wondering whether they will be sent to war; there are old men, and even some old women, deciding this for them.

Others wait to hear whether those for whom they care will be sent away to fight in a foreign world or permitted the luxury of an almost-ordinary life.

These are days hacked out by axes, hours sliced into the consciousness of the world by politics and money and forces so large they seem inhuman.

But there are also other moments, other kinds of waiting, other sorts of realizations. The huge catastrophic times live side by side with the quotidian.

As I type these words onto the computer screen, with one of my cats sprawled more or less on top of the keyboard and the other basking under the slight but definite heat given off by the old brass desk lamp, I know somewhere there is a person checking voice-mail, breathless with hope and trepidation, to hear whether the job offer came through. Despair waits alongside; so does promise.

Somebody else is waiting to hear whether the check cleared; another waits to find out whether the tests were negative; a third wonders, helpless, whether all the paperwork was finally processed correctly.

Me? I am doing what I do every week: making my deadlines and worrying my own worries. I would like to say that I have been able to put my petty concerns aside because, with such important matters on the horizon, my own have been swept away. They haven't been; I am not unselfish. Fretting and prowling and grinding my teeth, I am waiting to hear if I'll receive the grant I applied for a few months ago. The powers-that-be have already put the letters in the mail and yet I must still wait.

I thought I could avoid this particular craziness because I know better.

You see, I imagined I could apply and let my hope go, like a kite, into the wild blue and be content with whatever decision was made. I thought I could distance myself sufficiently—be mature. "You are way too old," I told myself, "to wait for validation like a dog listening for the footsteps of the master. If you're lucky, great, and if you're disappointed, you'll be no worse off than you are now."

That last part is the cheat. I was doing myself a disservice to think I'd be able to separate the attempt to win from the appetite to win. What's the worst that can happen? Nothing terrible. I will still have my job, and I will still have my writing. It is not as if I won't complete the book I discussed in the proposal. I'll keep doing what I do because I believe my work is important.

What's the best that can happen? It would be nice to have my writing underwritten, so to speak, by a grant. It would be like getting enthusiastically praised by your own family. (There, now I've jinxed it. Praise from those closest to you is hard to come by.)

And so I am keeping my fingers crossed in my own greedy heart for the possibility of my own good news even though I know that I should be giving whatever small trove of luck I have to those who need it more.

But luck, like love or airline tickets, is not transferable. It belongs to each of us individually.

Somewhere someone is slamming the door on a marriage, a woman is discovering she is pregnant, a woman is discovering she is not pregnant, a man is deciding this will be his last drink, a man is deciding this will be his last cigarette, someone is being really kissed for the first time.

Hanging in suspended animation, our small lives almost disappear against the light of global events. Yet these incidents, never truly incidental, alter the course of destiny one by one, moment by moment.

69

Five Reasons to Hate Twilight

1. The *only* real reason young women like *Twilight* is because of Edward. That is sad.

Why? It's sad because vampire Edward is *not* whom you want to end up with, especially for eternity.

Stuck with Edward's family in a sunless, airless, dull mansion, having conversations that hint at the possibility of ancient patterns of potential incest now repressed, not having sex, and eating game meats? It would be like being married to an Englishman but without the cute accent or the trace amounts of humor.

Also, after 119 years shouldn't Edward be out of high school already? Give the boy a Kaplan program. Let him crack 1000 in his SATs by the forty-seventh time and get the kid into a community college somewhere.

2. Let's get back to the sex, or lack of it, which is what hooks girls on the first volume: female readers love that Edward sleeps beside Bella and apparently only wants to kiss her neck.

Why do they like that? Because most real live (i.e., not dead, not 100-year-old-plus) guys who come within touching distance (so to speak) spend their time lunging almost randomly at breasts and buttocks. The amateur kisses of actual boys taste of gum and burritos, and they breathe audibly through their noses while they slip their tongues down the girls' throats like they're lizards hunting for flies.

They are most decidedly not doing what Meyer's Bat Boy does in the all-important thirteenth chapter of the first book, in the passage that makes girls gasp with delight and cross their legs even if they don't know why: "[H]e simply bent his face to mine, and brushed his lips slowly along my jaw, from my ear to my chin, back and forth. I trembled."

Actual boys are not models of aloof, self-contained self-control; they are like Labrador retrievers. Girls should be aware of the fact that when they encounter an immaculately groomed, perfectly manicured, impeccably dressed, polite, restrained young man who initially avoids their company when paired with them during science lab, what they have not met is the man of their dreams. What they have met is their new best gay male friend.

3. We should be appalled by Edward because Edward takes away Bella's keys to her very own car saying, "You're intoxicated by my very presence," whereupon she says—wait for it—"There was no way around it; I couldn't resist him in anything."

How nuts is this? Lamb Chop the puppet showed more backbone than this "Lamb" does!

How about if Bella kept her own keys—and her own integrity—and drove away from the narcissistic bastard?

By the way, the runner-up for this position was a line from an earlier chapter where Bella exclaims, "I couldn't imagine anything about me that could be in any way interesting to him."

For all those folks who say we're in a post-feminist generation: guess we still have a teensy bit of work on the whole self-esteem-building business for our girls, yes?

4. Back to the self-description of the characters as specific members of the food chain: girls, remember that if you're the lamb and he's the lion, you may lie down together, but you're still an entree.

5. Drumroll, please, as we get to the finale: "About three things I was absolutely positive. First, Edward was a vampire. Second, there was a part of him—and I didn't know how potent that part may be—that thirsted for my blood. And third, I was unconditionally and irrevocably in love with him."

(That line is on page 195—although, curiously enough, when the passage is quoted on the back cover of the trade paperback "potent" is changed to "dominant," and I bet we can imagine why.)

So the *big* reason to loathe *Twilight*? Fear of your lover should not be an aphrodisiac. Ever.

Let's sum up, shall we? Why is *Twilight* scarier for a grown-up woman than it is for a younger one?

Because we understand the implications.

Because we know that even as a romantic fantasy, it's a damaging one; that even for a trashy book, it's a lousy one; and that even—or especially—as an escape for a young woman who's longing to break out of her everyday confinements, it's a trap.

70

Fifty Shades of Stupefaction

How did we go from Lesley Gore belting out "You Don't Own Me," in 1963—a song that includes the line "Don't tie me down 'cause I'd never stay"—to the point where Ana Steele, the protagonist from *Fifty Shades of Grey* who appears more than fifty years later, can say, "Why do I want to spend every single minute with this controlling sex god? Oh yes, I've fallen in love with him," as she's being belted in—or tied up?

You've heard about *Fifty Shades of Grey*, right? It's all over the place, like something nasty on the bottom of your shoe.

Fifty Shades is truly a form of residue: it's what's left over when you extract the intelligence, wit, energy, and originality from a book.

The movie is based on a book, which itself was based on a blog, which was actually written as fan fiction for a novel called *Twilight* in which feminine subjugation, abjection, and erasure of the feminine self are central.

I'm not kidding, either.

Twilight, you'll remember, is the book where a girl falls in love with a vampire who's maybe ninety-seven years old but still in high school.

Anyway, in *Twilight* the girl becomes a vampire because her main squeeze is one. You know how it is: The woman always takes on the man's status. He's poor, she's poor; he's rich, she's rich; he's a bloodsucker, she's a bloodsucker.

And yet somehow *Fifty Shades of Grey* manages to make *Twilight* look like a feminist manifesto.

Frankly, it makes *I Hope They Serve Beer in Hell* and *American Psycho*—two seriously misogynist bestsellers—look like women-friendly works.

Fifty Shades of Grey associates masculinity with lots of money. We're talking billionaire-before-thirty wealth, not a-steady-job-with-benefits money. It associates femininity with shackles. We're talking literal, not metaphorical, shackles.

But the metaphorical ones are there, too. The twenty-two-year-old woman from *Fifty Shades* is instructed by her rich older boyfriend about what to wear: "I may need you to accompany me to functions, and I want you dressed well." In 1963, Lesley Gore insisted that when she was out with a date, he was absolutely not going "to put [her] on display. " That was an important line in 1963 because we were establishing that women were not things, right? Because women are not objects?

But in *Fifty Shades* becoming an object is actually the ambition held by the college-graduate female protagonist; she enjoys feeling "[l]ike a receptacle—an empty vessel to be filled at his whim."

You know, like an ashtray.

Her rich guy's philosophy of life is cribbed from CliffsNotes on Andrew Carnegie. Unable to formulate his own ideas, he repeats Carnegie, as if having learned the words phonetically: "A man who acquires the ability to take full possession of his own mind may take possession of anything else to which he is justly entitled."

So she is "anything else." Awww. Clearly the term will figure largely as an endearment on this year's Valentine's Day cards: "To

My Anything Else, to Which I Am Justly Entitled." And there will be a picture of bunnies hugging.

He didn't even say "To Whom." She is an "It."

Too bad the rich guy—Christian Grey—didn't get to the part where Carnegie writes: "There is little success where there is little laughter." Grey is singularly humorless and proud to describe himself as a "hopeless joke teller."

A moody sadist who doesn't like to be touched and can't tell a joke and about whom the female protagonist says "[h]e wants to hurt me. He says he'll think about my reservations, but it still scares me"—this is the new yummy?

I've written about similar issues before: The celebration of violence or the threat of violence, contorted and idealized into something "romantic," remains unsavory to me. Whether manufactured by men or by women, the product is an anathema.

Perhaps I'm beating a dead horse. It's still better than beating a live woman and calling it love.

71

Good Dirty Books Versus Bad Dirty Books

A hundred years of the women's movement and what do we have? Not only do we have *Twilight*. We have grown-up women sneaking off to read "mommy porn" on their Nooks.

Wouldn't our suffragette grandmothers be proud?

We've already talked about *Fifty Shades of Grey*. Despite what most men might think, this terribly popular title has very little to do with encouraging its readers to let their hair revert to its natural color.

Guys who think this novel will prevent their wives from going to the beauty parlor are kidding themselves. If anything, the opposite is true: women are going to the salon so that they can meet other women to discuss sadomasochism and dominance while complaining the water is too hot as a stylist shampoos them out.

Notice that women reading the book are not attempting to look better or become more seductive for the actual men in their lives. The actual men in their lives have become props; they are far less significant than the passage held by the bookmark.

Women are swatting away their small children in order to finish the sexy bits, of which there are many (actually, there's nothing else). They are staying in their sweatpants and ordering General

Tso's three times per week instead of cooking, going to work, or fulfilling their "Literacy in America" volunteer commitments.

Why? Apparently the majority of twenty-first-century women are now fantasizing about the tortured—and torturing—hero of *Fifty Shades of Grey*. My bet is that wealthy, virile, jet-owning men aren't exactly thumbing through the text because they're thumbing, umm, *The Wall Street Journal*. (You thought I was going to say something else, didn't you?)

Not that there's anything wrong with powerful men. Some are sort of cute. Even the ones who aren't cute often exude an intriguing mix of power, charm, and *savoir faire* (French for "expensive car") that explains their attraction for naïve women. Such guys might especially appeal to a significantly younger woman within their circle of influence even when their allure is starting to fade. Think Henry Kissinger. Think Yoda.

Women are encouraged by our culture to look for men who will provide them with an identity, even if that identity is "slave." The more prominent and elevated a man, the more difficult it is to secure his recognition, and so the more valuable his attention becomes. This sort gives women, especially insecure women, a sense that they are somebody if the powerful man knows their name, their tastes, or wears their ties—or makes them wear his.

It's as if such women are invisible until a powerful man looks in their direction and then they have achieved what they've always wanted: a name for themselves as so-and-so's latest object of desire. It used to be that the name women wanted from these relationships was wife, but that is no longer the case.

And I don't think we've moved up a notch, either.

Just when we thought our collective daughters' futures would be defined by stronger positions in the worlds of the culture, the workplace, the family, and politics, it turns out that a lot of women are soaking up this message, "You want me to make choices? OK, then! I am choosing to be submissive to a man who has a playroom of pain and who wants to decide what I eat, where I go, and purchases my electronic devices."

Do we really want to keep underscoring the lesson that women will obey you if (1) cash is dangled in front of them; and (2) they are treated poorly emotionally and physically?

Women are pretending that they are the virginal heroine (with the all-too common name of Anastasia Steele—don't you know, like, twelve women with that name?) whom he chooses as his object of desire.

Except "desire" is maybe not the right word for it: maybe "target" or "victim" would be more accurate.

And maybe "bondage" is a just sexy word for "degradation."

Which is not to say that there aren't some fabulous dirty books in this world.

I remember picking up a paperback of Anaïs Nin's *Delta of Venus* at King's Cross train station in London in the late 1970s. The book was new, having just been reissued shortly before Nin's death in 1977, but the stories had been written in the 1940s for a dollar a page; an editor had to convince Nin that the world was now ready to read in the light what she'd written in the shadows and indeed the book hit the best-seller lists for thirty-six weeks.

I knew nothing of that. All I knew was that Nin was a writer I'd heard of—one of a vast tribe of women writers from the 1920s, '30s, and '40s whom I was making it my job to get to know—but had no clue what kind of stories I'd be reading on my journey to Cambridge University, where I was a graduate student at the time.

More than thirty years ago, I still remember that particular train ride.

I simply could not believe what I was reading: I was blushing, squirming, giggling, and certain that every other proper, tweedy British passenger just knew I was seeped in porn.

Make no mistake: porn is what Nin had written. Gorgeous, lyrical, hot, sexy, beautifully crafted filth was at the heart of every tale.

I bought Nin's other book of dirty stories, *Little Birds*, for my return trip to London the next weekend.

Nin nailed our most compelling and subterranean drives. She wrote: "I, with a deeper instinct, choose a man who compels my strength, who makes enormous demands on me, who does not doubt my courage or my toughness, who does not believe me naïve or innocent, who has the courage to treat me like a woman." The whole power imbalance of fantastical, almost-mythical sexual situations is what she did best.

And my best bet is that Anaïs Nin would have flung *Fifty Shades of Grey* across the floor and said, "Who are you kidding, honey? If you're going to read filth, read well-written, smart, sexy, and good filth."

Consider Nin's "[h]e was now in that state of fire that she loved. She wanted to be burnt" or "I stroke it gently, gently, and I say, 'The little silver fox, the little silver fox. So soft and beautiful. Oh, Mary, I can't believe that you do not feel anything there, inside. She seems on the verge of feeling, the way her flesh looks, open like a flower, the way her legs are spread. Her mouth is so wet, so inviting, the lips of her sex must be the same."

Now compare these passages to E L James' "Why is anyone the way they are? That's kind of hard to answer. Why do some people like cheese and other people hate it? Do you like cheese?" or "My inner goddess jumps up and down with cheerleading pom-poms shouting yes at me."

Is the triumphant cry of the next generation of literate women really going to be "I don't care how rotten the writing is as long as it's entertaining" *and* "Anastasia didn't sign the sexual contract!"? Is that what a hundred years of the women's movement and excellent critical thinking have prepared as the rallying cry of the educated twenty-first-century female?

At least Nin's characters were complicated. All anybody who feels a need to defend James' hero can say is: "He was vulnerable and hid his own distress under his compulsion to offer pain!"

As we say in Brooklyn (I might have a degree from Cambridge, but I still talk like I'm from Coney Island), pull the other one. But unlike Anastasia, we are not saying it literally. You pull something on us, and we'll smack you.

Anaïs Nin knew better than to pretend her characters are "in love" or "heal each other" or "live happily ever after" in a room of pain decorated as a playpen. (Hey, has anybody wondered what the kids of Christian and Anastasia are going to be like? Want your kids to be in their play group?)

Anaïs Nin knew better than to believe that a guy watching you do things in various outfits only after you ask his permission and then regarding that as an act of "love" is not something helping us embrace earned trust, shared experiences, and happy, equally balanced sexual partnerships.

And she would have known that the only way *Fifty Shades of Grey* could possibly be satisfying in any respect would be for the masochistic reader who feels terrible prose is punishment.

72

Essential Must-Not-Reads

It is a truth universally acknowledged that many of the most successful contemporary books are not always the best contemporary
books, and this explains why many midlist authors believe there is
no God.

Selling by the thousands every day, however, are those volumes
focused on seventeen-year-old narrators whose most profound accomplishment is that they shoplifted, stole antidepressants from
their mother's stash, and had sex in an empty apartment all at the
same time. Like who hasn't? And these books treat shape-shifting
vampires as if they are any different from the guys we dated from
1978 to 1996. Even the hair is the same. Please.

What follows is a sampling of titles I will *not* be buying. Enjoy!

**Diet Book: *Just Lick It! How to Order Everything You Love to
Eat but Never Gain Weight!***

Have other diets left you so hungry that you bite at people's
shins as they walk by? Penned by the best-selling author of *Ladies,
Lard, and the Lord: The Surprisingly Spiritual Connection Between
the Cosmos and Colonic Cleansing,* this new work will have you
dropping pounds *and* getting dates with emotionally exotic men

who otherwise would have never looked at you had you not been working hard on spicing up the kale!

Non-Fiction/How-To: *The Smug Mothering Guide*

The theoretical and political assumptions that inform a sophisticated woman's sense of her life once she enters into Motherhood are explored sensitively and extensively in chapters such as "Have You Knit Their Sandals Yet?" and "Why I Make My Child's Water from Scratch." Chapters on the wisdom of choosing principles from Sun Tzu's *The Art of War* when applying to Dalton, Lawrenceville, Brearley, Eton, and Harrow, or other private schools make this a must-read. Audiobook, narrated by Gwyneth Paltrow, available.

Blockbuster: *Pope Tarot's Heresy of the Pharaoh's Tomb*

Former FBI agent and recently ordained Jesuit Seamus Evans ("Father Green Eyes") teams up with former undercover C.I.A. asset Yassir Thassmababbe to handle an unearthed cache of treasures, including unexpired coupons for Bed Bath & Beyond, from the tomb of pharaoh Karmamn Ghia, the only Egyptian ruler to govern solely through the use of restraining orders. Soon to be a major motion picture starring Kevin Spacey, Emma Watson, and Miley Cyrus.

Literary Fiction: *Good Walls*

I used to work with tone-deaf kids and I got a real kick out of them, with their bad humming and all. But I also got a little too much inside their heads and some of their heads were scary places to be, especially when you have perfect pitch, which I do. I couldn't handle it and I didn't want to do it at the expense of myself, you know? I wanted to get my own act together and I figured that it was like putting on your oxygen mask before you help others. You don't want to die first, right? Nobody does. So I do drywalls right now. I'm enjoying working with people. Parts of this novel were first published in *Glimmer Train* under the title "An Indelicate Spackling"

Here Are the Runners-Up!

- *Eat, Purge, Love: A Model's Guide to Travel and Happiness*
- *The Joy of Zoning Laws: A Sensuous Guide to the Built Environment*
- *Fill Your Life by Digging Your Own Moat*
- *This Old Fart: A Guide to Renovating Your Long-Term Partnership*
- *I Feel Bad About My Scrotum*
- *Lose Your Shirt, but Save Your Ass!: A Guide to Fitness During the Recession*
- *Dr. Smirnoff's Guide to Operating Heavy Machinery*
- *A Mistress at Christmas: A Holiday Story for—Oh, Sorry, I Need to Take This Call. . . .*
- *Guaranteed Tricks for Making a Good Confession*
- *Feckless!*
- *Self-Deception and You*
- *The Blithely Unconcerned: How to Achieve Happiness by Sticking Your Fingers in Your Ears*
- *Gambling Your Tuition: An Undergraduate's Guide*
- *Fun with Moccasins*
- *Puppies and Espresso: What to Give Your Stepchildren Before They Return Home*
- *Inuit Intuition: An Eskimo Shaman Teaches You How to Unfreeze Your Emotional Igloo*
- *How to Find Love on a Bus*
- *What CEOs Know That You Don't, or How to Inherit Wealth and Forge Business Relationships Through Prep School Connections*

- *The Duct Tape Diet*
- *How to Find a Feeble Man: Dating Tips for the Woman Who Has Simply Given Up*
- *Absolutism: The Philosophy of Vodka*
- *The Idiot's Guide to Refrigerator Magnets*
- *The American Boy Book of First Mandate Stories*
- *How to Dress like a Long Island Parking Lot Attendant (11–4 Shift)*
- *Only God Can Make Topiary: Inspiration by (or in) the Yard*
- *Viagra: A Pop-Up Book!* (*Not appropriate for readers under 50 or those without insurance*)
- *Wax Your Way to Happiness*
- *The Tragedy of Color Blindness: One Man's Nightmarish Descent into Conflicting Plaids* (illustrated)
- *Right Turns Only: A Guide to Washington*
- *The Enema of Enlightenment*
- *Virginia Werewolf: The Blood Curse of Bloomsburg*
- *Weaving Life's Lanyards of Despair: Tales from Summer Camp*
- *Cult Life: How to Hypnotize Your Readers into Buying Your Books in Bulk*

OK, OK: so I might still be tempted to purchase this last title. . . .

73

My Bikini Bridge Is the Verrazano

When you're thinking about bathing suit season, do me a personal favor, OK? Start appreciating your body before you start disrespecting it. Your body—including your thighs, your upper arms, your stomach, and your tush—is not your enemy.

When somebody asks you whether you're feeling good about heading to the beach, don't make a sad face while grabbing them by the wrist and explaining the concept of "back fat."

Tell them you can't wait for summer because you're going to slather yourself in sunscreen and head toward the water, wearing something comfortable to keep the sand out while keeping seagulls and cops away. That's all a bathing suit needs to do.

If somebody has the nerve to ask how you feel about the way you look, tell them that your pituitary gland is drop-dead gorgeous and that, despite everything, your liver's still functioning. Tell them you enjoy "looking within."

Celebrate those parts of your body that keep you going. The rest are best left quietly to deal with themselves.

If you hate your body enough to talk trash about it constantly, just imagine how it's tempted to react to you. You want to talk to your body the way the late, great Joan Rivers talked about trashy starlets in bad outfits? You think that's the way to have a healthy relationship with either your inner or your outer self?

You say enough nasty stuff about your upper arms, they'll start aching every time you pick up that 400-pound purse you insist on dragging everywhere. Soon, in solidarity, your elbows and ankles will receive the upper arms' memo and start protesting. They might develop just a touch of arthritis or arthritis-like symptoms to prove their point.

When I was talking with other women about how we might best go about refusing to let swimsuits sink our self-esteem, I came across a new concept that made all the other vanities seem almost benign.

Have you heard about the "bikini bridge"? No, it's not a little polka-dotted applique for your dental work; we should have only been so lucky.

A bikini bridge is defined as "[w]hen a thin woman who has a flat or concave stomach"—that's when I initially stopped reading, but kept going—"lies down, her bikini bottom should be suspended across her sculpted hipbones, leaving a shadowy gap."

Ha-ha-ha, whew, ha-ha. Why can't they come out and say: "If you're a woman over 30 or you weigh more than an even 100 pounds, please wear a full-body hazmat suit while approaching any beach, park or, not to put too fine a point on it, public area."

My bikini bridge would, of course, be the Verrazano. It's got twelve lanes, takes E-ZPass, and has a sign saying: "Life Is Worth Living."

I'm not even kidding.

Then I started thinking about how "bikini bridge" sounded like a title, as in "Bikini Bridge over the River Cry."

Professor Chad Stanley at Wilkes University suggested "Bikini Bridge over Troubled Waters" and a pal from Texas thought

"Bikini Bridges of Madison County" would work, but only if Meryl Streep used her Italian accent.

But whose attention are we hoping to get, really? Some random guy who strolls along the shore staring at women while they're napping, trying to get a glimpse of anatomical architecture? That'd be a great story to tell the children: "Your daddy loved my bikini bridge and that's why you're here."

The whole idea of girls and women striving to be desirable while not expressing desire isn't such a hot idea, no matter what the season.

Do you know the real reason we worry about how others think we look at the beach? It's because of the unflattering remarks we're making in our own heads about other people.

That is where this starts—and that's where we can help it end. Be generous instead of "judgey."

Instead of *tsk-tsking* in a sanctimonious whisper, "Whoever told her she'd look good in *that*?" we could think, "There's somebody who enjoys her food! I wanna sit next to her!"

Don't say it because you'd look better in comparison, either; say it loud because it's the truth.

That person will have the best picnic on the beach.

And that's how to start a fun summer.

EPILOGUE

What Everyone Must Stop Doing Right Now

1. Right this minute, everybody needs to stop chanting that blueberries are healthy and full of antioxidants. The next person who announces this gets his or her nose poked with a fork. Please stop insisting that everybody join the blueberry cult. Yes, blueberries are fruit. Yes, they are cute. Yes, they are nature's M&Ms. But that's it. Enough already with the blueberries. (I carry the fork on me at all times; be aware that the tines may sting.)

2. If you are sitting next to a person who is driving, do not take a sharp intake of breath to indicate danger when another car passes too close or looks as if it might stop short or when the driver is turning into her garage. This is not helpful, nor does it promote safety. It annoys and therefore shortens tempers and attention spans.

3. Do not say to any person who is more than eleven pounds overweight, "Salads are delicious!" That person already feels overweight and does not need to hear about salads or, even worse, smoothies. Hearing about leafy greens (or a certain berry

we won't discuss) will only make the other person unhappy and be forced to order a sea salt caramel sundae with extra whipped cream as consolation.

4. Do not give replaceable lovers irreplaceable gifts. Offer to others only what you can afford to lose.

5. Stop telling people that the hardest thing you do is not hard. Whether that is raising twins, maintaining a cheese-free diet, running triathlons, creating the perfect wildflower garden, balancing in three-inch heels, or writing an exquisite book, you know it isn't easy. If somebody compliments you on your perseverance, stamina, and talent, accept the comment with grace and gratitude. Do not diminish yourself or the other person by explaining how you do it in your sleep or while making fruit smoothies, which, by the way, are full of healthy ingredients.

6. Do not gawk at the poor soul who has been pulled over by the police. The poor soul is having a bad day.

7. Do not think it is OK for you to text at the table, at the wheel, at a meeting, at a wedding, at the movies, at a wake, or on a date. Even if you're making eye contact and have that weird vacant smile people plaster on their faces while their thumbs are doing Riverdance, it irritates others.

8. Even when you speak ironically and with cool hipness about dumb TV shows you watch, you are still making conversation about dumb TV shows. Switch to another topic.

9. Talking about dumb TV shows is still better than talking about your most recent physical ailment. Yes, people would rather hear your opinion concerning *Wife Swap* than listen to a detailed report concerning your recent visit to the gastroenterologist.

10. Don't throw your gum out the window. Somebody will step in it or a bird will eat it and die. Gum lasts longer than any other substance in the universe. After Armageddon, the only things that will be left are roaches and gum.

11. Do not ask how lesbians have sex. If you don't know, it's none of your business.

12. Don't be late. If you're going to be late, get in touch before the moment you are meant to arrive.

13. Don't assume that your ex, your siblings, your parents, your high school classmates, or your former colleagues have precisely the same memories you do.

14. Don't assume a plant is a good gift.

15. Don't be anybody's fool. Sometime it's appropriate to pick up your hat, say your good-byes, and go—taking with you the small amount of goodwill and dignity you have left.

16. Don't repeat compliments offered to you by salespeople. Salespeople are trying to make a commission, and saying to your startled friends, "But the personal shopper said I looked absolutely fabulous in orange knit!" will only make them feel shy in front of you and need to lower their eyes.

17. Stop taking pennies from the register if you don't really need them or if—especially if—you never put any in yourself.

18. Stop saying, "Oh, it's only me!" Stop putting the word "only" in front of yourself as something to hide behind, like a veil or a fan, as if it's girlie-cutesy. And that's not just my girlish way of looking at things, either. "Only You" is a great oldies song, but automatically saying, "It's only me," is no way for a grown-up to talk about herself.

19. Stop saying, "I just wanted to say that . . ." That's another automatic apology that has got to go, folks. Just say what it is you just want to say. Don't preface it with a thirteen-second introduction: spit it out, honey. It'll feel much better and, since life is short, you need to spend your time saying the important lines with finesse and aplomb.

20. Stop saying, "It's fine. Don't worry about me. I'll be OK with it, even though it's not what I'd originally planned or anything." Let's leave our evil friend, Passive Aggressive Whiner, in the dust. If you don't want to accept something, make your "no" emphatic and take responsibility for your action. If you are willing to be flexible, then do it without feeling sorry for yourself.

21. Stop telling yourself, "This has got to change," and then doing nothing because "I'm only one person." We all have our own version of a significant issue that's too overwhelming, too enormous, too intimidating, and apparently too far away from our own sphere of influence to do anything except break our hearts or make us furious and frustrated. We wring our hands and break our hearts, believing ourselves powerless. That is the first thing that needs to change. We have to take away the word "only." We have to turn the phrase "I'm one person" into a battle cry and a cheer of encouragement. You're a woman, a citizen, a person of conviction. You have courage, a voice, and a vote: go make some trouble.

22. Tomorrow is promised to no one—not even those who subsist on a diet entirely of blueberries. Enjoy yourself right this minute. Start now.

ACKNOWLEDGMENTS

My marvelous editor at St. Martin's, Michael Flamini, makes every-thing better: books, conversations, lunches, and life are all im-proved when he's involved. The smartest and funniest parts of this collection—especially its title—are sharper and fiercer because of him. My agent, Deborah Schneider, sharp and fierce herself, insisted that I write with more honesty and less glibness, going for the heart as well as the funny bone; leaning on (but never in) her and drawing from her endless courage, Deborah encouraged me into more personal territory than I'd dared enter previously. To Michael and Deborah, my deepest thanks.

Vicki Lame, associate editor at St. Martin's, makes the work of turning manuscript-into-book seem effortless, which translates into "Vicki Lame is magic." To Vicki I owe more than I dare ad-mit; it's a Rumplstilskin kind of thing and my own fear is that someday Ms. Lame may want to collect—and there will never, could never, be enough.

I refer to my assistant, Kristina Dolce, as KDTM for "Kissy Dolce, The Magnificent" and even that doesn't do her justice. For three years, she's sat in my basement office at the University of Connecticut, helping me invent, revise, and rework my writing even as she completed her M.A. in English literature and taught her own classes. Reading the manuscript at every stage, Krissy has been both my inspiration and my gatekeeper; she has been both audience and critic. To Krissy goes my gratitude and with her I split my sense of accomplishment.

Pam Katz, author, screenwriter, professor, and best of friends through everything, also read the whole damn thing several times. For her pains, her reward was to be harangued by my worries, fears, and anxieties about everything from word choice to whether or not I should get a professional cover photo. To Pam I owe a fountain of champagne at the Algonquin, my deep respect, and a lifetime of "Is this a good time to talk?" conversations on any topic of her choosing.

Niamh Cunningham Emerson, former student, friend, and emerging editor, gave the manuscript a thorough examination and made me proud: if I had anything to do with teaching her to read closely and well, it paid off. She helped enormously. So did Erica Buehler, an undergraduate who, new to the work, did a final line edit and saw places needing spit-shines that the rest of us (too familiar with the prose to see anything) had missed. That young woman has a great future ahead of her.

Laura Rossi Totten, another UConn graduate turned brilliant professional, has been my publicist and handler for years; her patience is legendary and her enthusiasm is as contagious as it boundless. She knows I owe her because I tell her "I OWE YOU, LAURA" when things go well. If things go well (and they usually do) it's because Laura had a hand in it.

Heidi Calderwood Rockefeller has kept our house clean for twenty-four years. Heidi deserves not only acknowledgments but a medal: without her I wouldn't be able to write on Fridays because I'd would be cleaning the bathrooms, mopping the floors, and trying to make a bed while the cats try to get into the pillowcases (as they always do). As a voracious reader of both fiction and nonfiction, it's Heidi who usually hears the first lines of an essay. "Does this make sense?" I'll trail around the house asking her as she dusts around books. "I think you're avoiding the real topic," Heidi will reply as she fluffs a duvet, or say, "That sounds an awful lot like what you wrote about last year." She knits me socks and keeps me in her prayers. Her gifts are unparalleled.

Carolyn Lumsden at *The Hartford Courant* told me I could write columns for them; when Carolyn tells me I've done a good job, my heart sings (usually in Italian). Peter Pach, as my weekly editor, does the heavy lifting, making sure the words fit together and fit on the page. The Tribune Company permits the columns to go around the world and allows readers from South Dakota, Dubai, and Otago, New Zealand, to keep me busy answering mail. Hara Estroff Marano at *Psychology Today* not only makes my blogs for the *PT* site better but makes me feel better about myself, which is not part of her work as the magazine's executive editor or as its advice columnist.

There's my own extended #TribeofLoudSmartWomen, the ones who keep me laughing and keep me going: Faith Middleton of The Faith Middleton Food Schmooze; Roxanne Coady of RJ Julia Booksellers; Teresa Younger of the Ms. Foundation for Women; Patti Russo of the Women's Campaign School at Yale University; Teri Rivza of the Erma Bombeck Writers Workshop; Amy Hartl Sherman of "Kranky Kitty" cartoon fame; who came up with the chapter title for Part 5; Gianetta Palmer of "Reflections of a Middle-Aged Fat Woman"; Barbara "Beloved" Cooley of "Your Life and Times"; Kari Lynn "Bangs" Collins at the *Iowa Park Leader;* Margaret Peterson, Bonnie Jean Feldcamp, Astra Groskaufmanis, and Mandy Smith Brasher.

Thanks for listening to all these stories the first time around go to Bonnie Januszewski, Nancy Lager, Tim Taylor, Gerry and

Acknowledgments

Fleur Lawrence, Laney Greenberg, Mona and Todd Friedland, Lynette Lager, Inda Watrous, Margaret Mitchell, Kerri Brown, Jay Heinrichs, Ines Kramer, David Hanley and my brother, Hugo Barreca Jr. You laugh in the right places and tell me if the words work well.

And for saving the last class for me, the last dance, the last kiss good-night as well as the first kiss good-morning, for keeping me safely in the banana boat of love (see chapter 23), I save the last and best thanks for my husband, Michael Meyer.

I am a lucky girl. Yes, I am.